The
CASSEROLE QUEENS
MAKE-A-MEAL
Cookbook

The CASSEROLE QUEENS MAKE-A-MEAL Cookbook

Mix and Match 100 Casseroles, Salads, Sides, and Desserts

CRYSTAL COOK & SANDY POLLOCK

CLARKSON POTTER/PUBLISHERS
NEW YORK

Published in the United States by Clarkson Potter/Publishers, an imprint of the
Crown Publishing Group, a division of Random House, Inc., New York.
www.crownpublishing.com
www.clarksonpotter.com

CLARKSON POTTER is a trademark and POTTER with colophon is a registered
trademark of Random House, Inc.

Library of Congress Cataloging-in-Publication Data
Cook, Crystal.
   The casserole queens make-a-meal cookbook: mix and match 100 casseroles,
salads, sides, and desserts / Crystal Cook and Sandy Pollock. — First edition.
      pages cm
   Includes index.
1. Casserole cooking.   I. Pollock, Sandy.   II. Title.
   TX693.C645 2013
   641.82'1—dc23   2012046898

ISBN 978-0-7704-3680-3
eISBN 978-0-7704-3681-0

Printed in the United States of America

Book and cover design by Rae Ann Spitzenberger
Cover photographs by Ben Fink

10 9 8 7 6 5 4 3 2 1

First Edition

*"All too often, our ambition consumes us,
and leads to hasty decisions. An intelligent spouse
can help refine and focus that drive."*
—JACQUELINE KENNEDY

This book is for Michael Lovitt
and Tim Tankersley. Thank you for keeping
us focused throughout our casserole journey!
(And, yes, we know what a task that must be—
shiny objects are just so distracting!)

CONTENTS

the
CASSEROLE QUEENS
are back!

Hi, it's Crystal and Sandy, and we're back for a second helping! We're the Casserole Queens, two dear friends who are proudly front and center of a growing casserole movement. We, along with thousands of other folks across the country, are reviving this American mealtime staple with fresh ingredients and updated flavors. Of course, we like to throw in some kitsch and retro-chic style, to keep things fun with a nod to the 1950s, when casseroles reigned supreme. But these delightfully simple and wholesome dishes are truly timeless and are the best way to put a delicious, from-scratch meal on the table so that you can actually sit down with your family at the end of the day. As we kick off our second cookbook, we're taking the concept a step further, giving you great ways to add even more spontaneity and flair to your meals. So grab your quirkiest apron, grease up a casserole dish, and get ready for a fresh new batch of hot-from-the-oven goodness that'll have your family crowded around the table.

Let's Make-a-Deal to Make-a-Meal!

We love casseroles for the fact that you can get an entire meal out of one simple dish (they aren't called one-dish wonders for nothin'). Most casseroles are packed with all the wonderful flavors you need to satisfy everyone in your family, even the picky ones. But a good meal doesn't end there, and the Casserole Queens are always looking for ways to shake things up! We might like a nice, crisp salad to accompany a hearty baked pasta, or a homemade cornbread to complement a spicy Tex-Mex dish. And since we figured we weren't alone, we thought we'd jot it all down for you in this nice little book. So pick it up any time to help you mix-and-match your own menu and make a meal that you'll be proud of!

We've packed this book with forty-six casserole entrée recipes and fifty salads, sides, and desserts that break out of the 9 x 13-inch mold. Don't worry, our casseroles are always center stage—we can't help it! But that doesn't mean they have to stand alone. There's plenty of variety here for you to keep your loved ones interested, and maybe even excited, to sit down at the table. And that's just the point. Cooking and planning should be easy, so you can enjoy good time spent with family. Yes, it is possible. Make sure to look for our recommendations of what goes good with what, but feel free to make it your own! Here is just a taste of what you can expect to find—fresh, new ideas paired with the perfect recipe:

✳ *Entertainer Extraordinaire* Planning dinner for friends? In-laws? The big cheese? Try classic staples that will surely impress, such as our Chicken with 40 Cloves of Garlic with Carrot Soufflé and Asparagus Bundles Wrapped in Prosciutto. Just one of the many great ideas we have for easy, fun, and economical ways to entertain. (Maybe now will be a good time to ask the ol' boss for a raise.)

★ *Timely Favorites* If extra time is something you only dream about, then our chapter of recipes requiring just seven ingredients or fewer is for you! Try our Super-Simple Spinach-Stuffed Shells with Broccoli Rabe with Shallots for rumbling tummies. These recipes come together in a flash and are an easy way to get dinner on the table before the family starts giving you the stink-eye.

★ *Adventurous Palate* Throw your typical Tuesday night a curveball! Explore the wonders of our Moussaka plated with a side of our Tomato and Feta Salad for a true Mediterranean feast. We're setting out to show the world that there are casseroles for every type of connoisseur—so pack your favorite 9 x 13-inch dish, because we're going international, baby!

★ *No gluten? No meat? No problem!* Dietary restrictions don't have to mean casseroles can't be a part of your life. Pair our Rustic Polenta Casserole (packed with mushrooms, tomatoes, and ricotta cheese) with our Panzanella Salad for a delightful and filling vegetarian meal. We've made a conscious effort to address some of the dietary challenges that many of us have. In fact, you'll find an entire chapter especially devoted to helping you out in the kitchen. There's nothing like exciting, new recipes to make you feel good about your choices. You'll also find pointers for simple substitutions that can transform recipes to meet vegetarian, gluten-free, or even diabetic-friendly diets. See The Conscientious Casserole (page 12) for more information on these recipes.

You see, folks, casseroles are fun, retro, and exactly our thing, but that doesn't mean they're all we do. We're keeping dinner time interesting with a plethora of side dishes, salads, and dessert options to help round out your square table! So let's go make that meal! We promise to keep it simple and, most important, fun (we like fun).

The Conscientious Casserole: Food to Fit Your Lifestyle

First and foremost, we want to clearly state that the Queens are not doctors. Nor would anyone in their right mind ever want to cast us to play doctors on TV. So please note that this book is not intended to be a nutritional guide, and that you should have your doctor or nutritionist advise you as to what is best for you and your specific needs.

With that said, we've discovered that food allergies and intolerances are an ever-increasing concern in our Casserole Kingdom, so we wanted to address these challenges. Everyone is entitled to deliciousness! But first, we admittedly needed some education. We consulted with another fabulous Austin-area business woman, Carly Pollack, who owns a company called Nutritional Wisdom. There are a staggering number of issues that people can be faced with when choosing what to eat—so many, in fact, that it would be impossible to cover all of them. So we settled on the categories that we felt were most relevant to our fans: vegetarian, gluten-free, and diabetic-friendly.

Throughout the book, you'll find lots of recipes (all identified by helpful icons) that we developed with certain restrictions in mind, as well as tips for tweaking dishes to suit your needs with easy adaptations. Regardless of the restriction or substitution, we feel confident that these are dishes the entire family will enjoy.

Friendly Faces

I spy a helpful icon! Here's a guide to the memorable, helpful icons scattered throughout this book. At a quick glance, you will be able to identify which recipes are or can be made gluten-free, diabetic-friendly, or vegetarian with simple substitutions—as well as those that freeze well for use on another day. Now you know exactly what to look out for!

 FREEZES WELL!

 Gluten-free!

 Diabetic-friendly!

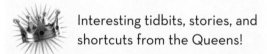 Vegetarian!

 Interesting tidbits, stories, and shortcuts from the Queens!

GLUTEN-FREE

To whip up gluten-free recipes, we got creative with ingredients like polenta, grits, rice, gluten-free pasta, and gluten-free bread. Some of our favorite gluten-free recipes in this book are:

- **Deconstructed Cabbage Rolls (aka Pigs Out of the Blanket)** (page 36)

- **Baked Sausages with Fennel** (page 48)

- **Rosemary Baked Ham** (page 78)

- **Rustic Polenta Casserole** (page 84)

- **Erin's Special Gluten-Free Corn Dog Casserole** (page 86)

- **Monterey Chicken and Rice** (page 102)

- **Mashed Potato Pizza** (page 104)

- **Pint-Size Caprese Salad** (page 126)

- **Crystal's May-I-Have-More-Mayo Potato Salad** (page 130)

- **Tomato, Goat Cheese, and Quinoa Salad** (page 137)

- **Brussels Sprouts with Bacon, Garlic, and Shallots** (page 146)

- **Nene's Spanish Rice** (page 153)

- **Granny Pansy's Baked Apples** (page 174)

Casserole Queens–Approved Gluten–Free Brands

With some simple substitutions, casseroles can easily be a part of a gluten-free diet. Hooray! Please remember: it is extremely important when cooking for people with gluten intolerances or wheat allergies that you either make your items from scratch or purchase products from a company that's committed to operating out of a gluten-free factory. Here are some of our top brand recommendations, backed by our favorite nutritionist, Carly:

- For a cracker topping, or if you simply want to add some character to your casserole, Mary's Gone Crackers brand makes a tasty cracker that packs a crunch. Also try good ol' Kellogg's Corn Flakes for a crunchtacular cereal topping.

- Pasta? Yes way! Choose from quite a few gluten-free options. We like Glutino, though we also like Ancient Harvest Quinoa Gluten-Free Pasta.

- Many commercial soup products contain gluten. For gluten-free, we reach for Pacific Natural, which offers cream of celery, cream of chicken, and cream of mushroom.

- There's even a simple swap for bread crumbs! Make your own using Rudi's Gluten-Free Bread or Udi's prebaked bread and our recipe for bread crumbs on page 188! You can find the breads in your grocer's freezer section. If it is a stuffing mix you need, try Aleia's Gluten-Free Savory Stuffing Mix.

- We think that the best ready-made gluten-free baking mix options are Pamela's Gluten-Free Baking Mixes, which come in varieties like flour, cookie, pancake, and brownie. Of course, we also love the flour mix recipe provided by nutritionist Carly and found on page 186. Not only does it work beautifully, but it is also high in fiber!

- If there is a dessert recipe that calls for a cookie crumble, Arrowhead Mills has an excellent variety of gluten-free cookies and snacks.

- Lots of our recipes call for condiments, sauces, or dressings. We do offer lots of substitution recommendations and from-scratch options, but we've found that Sass brand condiments and salad dressings are very good!

DIABETIC-FRIENDLY

The recipes with a diabetic-friendly icon were developed to drastically reduce or cut out grains and sugar (especially processed grains such as crackers, cereal, pasta, etc.). They also limit high-starch vegetables such as white potatoes, corn, and peas. Try these winning recipes:

- **Chicken with 40 Cloves of Garlic** (page 43)
- **Yvonne's Unstuffed Poblano Casserole** (page 58)
- **Shakshuka** (page 60)
- **Awesome Aussie Meat Pies** (page 70)
- **The Nelly Frittata** (page 91)
- **Butternut Squash Gratin with Asiago Cheese and Toasted Pine Nuts** (page 92)
- **Farro, Wild Mushroom, and Walnut Casserole** (page 94)
- **Tomato and Avocado Salad** (page 127)
- **Spinach and Spice and Everything Nice** (page 140)
- **Asparagus Bundles Wrapped in Prosciutto** (page 143)

VEGETARIAN!

For our vegetarians friends, we have developed lots of recipes that are free of red meat, poultry, fish, and seafood—yet are still comforting and satisfying. Some of our favorites include these:

- **Summertime Tomato Basil Pie** (page 80)
- **Cheesy Grits-Stuffed Eggplant Rolls with Tomato Sauce** (page 82)
- **Spinach and Gruyère Soufflé** (page 88)
- **Butternut Squash Gratin with Asiago Cheese and Toasted Pine Nuts** (page 92)
- **Broccoli Rabe with Shallots** (page 142)
- **Braised Endive Gratin** (page 147)
- **Carrot Soufflé** (page 150)
- **Risotto with Asparagus and Lemon** (page 152)
- **Royal Ratatouille** (page 154)

Now you can feel good about what you eat, and enjoy it just the same!

let the
GOOD TIMES
casserole

There are two things the Queens truly adore: great food and great company. Sounds dreamy, right? We have some fun entertaining ideas that will inspire you to cook up nights you'll never forget. With delicious new recipes and a game or craft, you'll not only get people to the table, but you'll also get them off their smart phones and engaged. Hey, little Susie, we'll give you somethin' to text about!

When's the last time you hosted a potluck? One surefire way to get people together is to make dinner a group effort. Hello, potluck, where have you been? Invite your family, your friends, their kids, even their neighbors' kids. With these recipes, you'll have plenty of potluck power to get them in the door. Making casseroles is inexpensive, serves plenty, and is having a comeback. Why order a pizza and watch reruns on TV when you can have great food and great times with all of your friends? Here are a few of our favorite ways to have a fabulous potluck.

The Casserole Queens Swap! Scandalous!

Let's face it, casserole fans! The idea of freezing make-ahead meals for a busy week sounds pretty much like a second job. Why not turn this potential chore into a party extravaganza by inviting friends over to sample and swap casseroles? What wonders you'll take home to your freezer! Cooking and freezing dishes for a casserole swap gives everyone some much-needed excitement in the kitchen. And wouldn't it be nice to cross one more thing off of your "to-do" list?

Casserole swaps are also ideal for helping others who could use an extra hand. Let's say someone in your group of friends is expecting a new baby. A "swap" can turn into a fun way to stock her freezer for those nights when the new parents are too tired to know what day it is. Whether it's an excuse to hang out with your BFFs or to stock your own freezer or a friend's, Casserole Queen Swaps are a novel way to save time, save money, and add some spice to your dinner preparation.

THE PREP

To ensure that there are a wide range of dishes to choose from, assign each guest a different casserole to bring. Since you are potentially providing others with meals for the week, you can choose from a variety of flavors to keep things interesting! Need ideas? Well, hot dog!, this book just happens to be full of them. Here is a sample menu idea, but we have lots of recipes that are highlighted with a "freezes well!" icon throughout this book. Find the ones that speak to you and go!

Sample Menu

- Macaroni-and-Beef Casserole (page 46)

- Yvonne's Unstuffed Poblano Casserole (page 58)

- The "Sitch" Chicken Parmesan (page 64)

- Chicken Paprikash (page 72)

- Cheesy Grits-Stuffed Eggplant Rolls with Tomato Sauce
  (page 82)

Each family and/or couple will cook two batches of their assigned casserole: one to freeze and swap, and one to enjoy at the party. (We found that approximately five families and/or couples work best since most people don't have more than one oven to keep the tasting casseroles warm.) This way, everyone gets to try each casserole and pick one to take home. Or if the goal of your get-together is to have more than just one additional meal on hand, you can cook more than two batches—it's easier to cook more of the same thing rather than cooking a gazillion different recipes.

THE SETUP

When setting up the swap, here are some important things to keep in mind:

- Assign casseroles with similar serving portions. It would be such a sad sight if Sally picked up a casserole that feeds eight, and Flo took home a casserole that feeds only two. Boo-hoo!

- Remind your guests that the best way to freeze a casserole is at the stage right before baking, when all the ingredients have already been prepped, cooked, and beautifully assembled in the pan. That way you'll get a freshly baked taste!

- Use disposable containers, such as aluminum pans. Clean-up will be a snap, and you don't have to worry about losing a dish! Also, look for pans with cardboard or flat aluminum tops, which take up less room in the freezer and stack better.

- Ask your guests to bring a recipe card, complete with baking or reheating instructions. It can easily be taped to the top of the casserole or cataloged into a recipe book. *Ding!* Party favor alert! Give your guests an empty photo album with 4 x 6-inch cards for them to start storing their recipes in. Wanna go the extra mile? Take a picture of the casserole for the opposite sleeve!

- If you are creating an entrée that should be served over rice or pasta, bring those extra dry ingredients in a plastic zip-top bag. It's simply the polite thing to do!

- With each guest bringing a frozen casserole, you might want to clear out some freezer space, or have everyone BYOC (Bring Your Own Cooler)!

THE DRINKS

Much like Crystal and Sandy, casseroles and cocktails are two great things that go together! What better way to make the whole event even more festive? Just take a quick inventory of the flavor of your dishes and get creative! Pitchers of margaritas or sangria are easy to mix up (see sidebar opposite) and work well with Mexican and Spanish dishes; a variety of wines pair nicely with Italian or French cuisine; and a dry martini can turn any swap into a formal affair. Now, cheers to you for pulling off a casserole swap without breaking a sweat!

RED, RED WINE SANGRIA

(Don't hate us for getting that song stuck in your head.)

Serves 6

½ cup sugar (for simple syrup)
1 bottle dry red wine (we prefer Spanish Rioja)
½ cup Spanish brandy
¼ cup fresh lemon juice
⅓ cup fresh orange juice
½ cup triple sec
1 lemon, sliced
1 orange, sliced
1 lime, sliced
Splash of ginger ale

1 Make a simple syrup by combining the sugar and ½ cup water in a small saucepan set over medium-high heat. Bring to a boil, reduce the heat to low, and simmer for about 2 minutes or until the sugar has dissolved. Let cool. The simple syrup may be made ahead and stored in an airtight container in the refrigerator for up to a month.

2 In a large pitcher or bowl, combine ½ cup simple syrup (or more to taste) with the wine, brandy, lemon juice, orange juice, and triple sec. Add the lemon, orange, and lime slices and stir. You can serve this immediately, adding a splash of ginger ale to each glass, but it's best if you refrigerate it overnight to let the flavors blend.

Game Nights . . .
Bring on the Bunco!

For a great game night, anything goes, really—Pictionary, dominos, cards, charades. But for the purpose of this book we are going to focus on a little game called Bunco! If it's good enough for the *Real Housewives of Orange County*, it's good enough for us! Seriously, though, to us, Bunco is not just a dice game, but a tradition. Sandy's mom has been a part of a Bunco group for more than forty years, and now her daughters are carrying on the custom. Young or old, Bunco rocks! If you are new to Bunco, here are a few tips:

- You will need at least four players. The more tables of four that you have, the more fun the game will be. Twelve players is ideal.

- Decide which set of Bunco rules you want to use for the group. You will find several different ideas for rules at www.buncogame.com/bunco-rules.

- Purchase the few items you need for the game—dice, a bell, score sheets, and enough pens to go around. Set up tables of four with pens and score sheets.

- Plan the menu. Keep it simple for your own sake. An example of an easy dinner would be a delicious baked dish from this book, and then everyone else could bring a side to complement it (well, heck—even those can come from this book)! Check out Sandy's favorite Bunco night side dish, Hargill's Bunco Club 7-Layer Salad, on page 129.

- Determine prizes. As the hostess, you will need three prizes: for first, second, and last places (also known as the booby prize). With twelve participants, each member can host one time a year and spread the hosting duties equally.

- **Most important:** Don't take the game too seriously. You could be shunned from the group if you are too much of a stickler for the rules. The game is far more social than actually competitive.

Just like our casseroles aren't your mama's casseroles, Bunco isn't your mama's bridge game.

We think Bunco has become popular in American culture because it's a good excuse for girl time. The rules are simple, the pace is high energy, and it's guaranteed fun. The best part is, the person with the most points at the end of the night usually takes home a prize. In some cases, like in Sandy's Hargill group, it's a booby! (Prize that is.)

Bunco started in England during the eighteenth century and made its way to the United States in 1855. Now more than 17.4 million American women play regularly, according to Procter & Gamble, who sponsored the first World Bunco Championship tournament in Las Vegas. With a $50,000 grand prize, this nationally televised event was a huge hit. But most women aren't playing for the competition or a hefty cash prize. They're playing to take a mental break from deadlines, dirty clothes, dogs, and dishes. They're playing to catch up with friends, family, and neighbors over good food and good laughs. It's easy to play at any age, and we haven't met a woman who didn't have a fun time.

If you throw a Bunco party featuring some of our tasty recipes, we'd love to see pictures! Send them to info@casserolequeens.com and we'll post them on our blog.

Craft Night! Introducing the Casserole Tote

So you're a casserole-baking pro . . . then you need the perfect tote in which to carry your casseroles. Lucky for you, we're about to get crafty. *Ding!* Party favor alert! Give your guests a savvy tote, made especially by you—it's a handmade gift that they'll actually use. (Pssst, we won't tell if you just want to keep the tote for yourself.)

Note that these instructions are for a tote that will comfortably fit a 9 x 13-inch casserole dish. Once you have the hang of making this tote, the size can always be modified to fit other casserole dishes. Although it's not necessary, we recommend using prequilted fabric, which helps to insulate and keep hot foods hot. Not sure what to do with your grandmother's unfinished quilt scraps? Sounds tote-worthy to us!

MATERIALS NEEDED

1 yard prequilted, reversible print fabric (see Note)

Scissors

2 (12-inch) straight purse handles, dowels, or bamboo handles

Straight pins

4 pieces sew-on Velcro (6 inches long and 1 inch wide)

Matching or coordinating thread

Note: If you want to create your own quilted fabric, place 1 yard of fabric face down. Layer 1 yard of Insul-Bright on top of this, and lay another yard of fabric on top, facing up. Quilt as desired. If opting for this technique, have fun with the patterns and mix and match. One layer will be seen on the outside of the carrier and the other as you open it.

All edges can be finished with a serger or with a zigzag or overcast stich for a more finished look.

(CONTINUES)

STEPS

1 You want to have one main piece and two side pieces for this project. Cut one main piece 36 x 16 inches. Cut two side pieces that are each 24 x 8 inches.

2 Take the two 24 x 8-inch side pieces, turn under and pin a ½-inch hem toward the center along both (long) sides, and stitch.

3 Take the 36 x 16-inch piece and, on the narrow ends, fold 2 inches from the end into the center and pin. You are going to cut out a semicircle for the handles. Using a bowl or plate that is 8 inches in diameter as a circular template, place your circle on the short side, so that it overlaps by about 4 inches deep and 8 inches across. Trace the curve of the bowl or plate where it meets the 2-inch fold. Cut out the semicircle formed by the curve of the template and the straight edge of the folded fabric. Once the fabric is unfolded, you will end up with a half-moon shape just below the 2-inch fold. Repeat on the other end.

4 Once you have cut out your handle cutouts, remove the pins. Finish the curved edges of the semicircle with a simple narrow stitch.

5 On the 36 x 16-inch piece, refold the edges down 2 inches, toward the center, and stitch along the serged edge to create a 2-inch hem/space for the handles. Repeat on both ends of the fabric. (Note that the purse handles are not inserted until the project is completed.)

6 Fold the 36 x 16-inch piece in half lengthwise so that handle cutouts are aligned. Mark the center on both sides with chalk or quilting markers. Fold the 24 x 8-inch pieces in half lengthwise and mark the center of each short end.

7 Match the center of the side of the 24 x 8-inch piece to the center of the 36 x 16-inch main piece, with the right sides together. Stitch the 24-inch side of the 24 x 8-inch piece to the 36-inch side of the 36 x 16-inch piece. Sew one side at a time, stopping 2 inches from the edge of the short side. Repeat with the second 24 x 8-inch piece on the other side. The two 24 x 8-inch pieces will extend away from the 36 x 16-inch piece, creating a flap on each side.

8 Place a 9 x 13-inch casserole dish in the center of the fabric to aid as a template. Fold the unsewn 2-inch pieces of the 24 x 8-inch piece toward its partner on the opposite side (this will create the end walls of the area where the casserole will sit).

9 Separate the sew-in Velcro. You will be sewing one side to each of the exposed 2-inch pieces, close to the edge and centered. If both edges are folded to the center, one will be on top and the other will be on the bottom. Check to see that they are placed correctly to hold the side flaps together before stitching. Once you have verified placement, stitch one-half of Velcro to each side flap.

10 Insert handles, bamboo, or dowels into the 2-inch hem. Enjoy!

Written sewing instructions can be tricky, so check our website, www.CasseroleQueens.com, for a step-by-step video demonstrating how to put it together.

Tips from the Casserole Queens' Kitchen

Cooking is easy and fun when you're prepared for the job at hand. Here are some helpful tips that we've gathered when working in our own kitchen that we hope will be handy in yours.

DECLUTTER YOUR CULINARY SPACE

Mise en place, people! *Voulez-vous* say what? *Mise en place* is a French term that means "everything in place." For cooks, it's a technique of organizing yourself, and it's simply the best time-saver out there—hands down! What you do is read through your recipe, prepare and measure out all of your ingredients, and put everything in its own bowl. Then you line up all of the equipment you're going to use. Preparing the *mise en place* ahead of time allows you to cook without having to stop and find things. Once you're all set up, putting a dish together is a snap!

CONTAIN YOURSELF!

Invest in some ramekins, Tupperware containers, zip-top baggies, and stackable mixing bowls. (The ten-piece glass set from Williams-Sonoma is Crystal's favorite!) They're very useful for preparing your *mise en place* and for just generally being ready to go. If you're dreading the dish mess afterward, simply reuse some of your plastic take-out containers or prepared grocery item tubs. Recycling is as easy as rinsing and putting it in the right bin!

THROW IN THE TOWEL

Head to your local restaurant supply store and buy a pack of absorbent cloth towels (nothing fancy or decorative) to have handy to wipe down surfaces and clean up spills. They are far more important for achieving ultimate kitchen Zen than one might think. And they're much more economical and eco-friendly than endless rolls of paper towels.

TO SAVE TIME WITH DISHES, THINK LIKE GROUPER FISHES!

Put like utensils in the same section of the silverware tray in the dishwasher—knives with knives, small forks with small forks, and so forth. That way, you can pull them out by groups and put them away just as fast. You can also do the same for similarly sized plates and bowls.

IT'S A SOAKER!

This is what we call those pesky pans with baked-on food because it takes a good soak before they can be cleaned. We have a handy tip for tackling such tricky messes faster than ever: set your dirty pots on the stove with some vinegar and water or dish soap and water, and then let them boil while you eat. By the time you finish dinner and get started on the dishes, the hot water solution will have loosened stuck-on food.

DO YOUR KNIVES MAKE THE CUT?

Good sharp knives make all the difference, but hold off on spending your entire paycheck on a prepackaged block set. You can get just about any job in the kitchen done with only an all-purpose chef knife, a paring knife, and a serrated knife (aka a bread knife). You'll also want a pair of kitchen shears, which are perfect for snipping twine, cutting flower stems, and trimming vegetables and meats.

If you're serious about cooking, then picking a knife is sort of like picking a mate. You will want to love it for life. When choosing a knife, pick it up and see how it feels in your hand. The weight and shape of the handle is important. How is the grip? Is it comfortable? Is it substantial enough without being too heavy? In addition to buying a good knife, you must also keep the edge sharp. Get a honing steel while you're at it, and ask the folks in the store to teach you how to use it.

GARLIC: PREPPING THE CLOVE
BEFORE IT HITS THE STOVE

Many great recipes call for garlic, and if it's all the same to you, buying jars of preminced garlic might be a real time-saver. But for those who feel allegiance to tradition, here are a few tips for some garlic peeling, prepping, chopping, and mincing techniques:

✳ *Peeling* If a recipe calls for multiple cloves at once, put them in a small resealable bag and hit the bag lightly with a jar or onto a hard surface. The peels will loosen right up. You can also microwave the cloves (not in a bag) for 10 to 15 seconds if the skins are especially tough to remove.

✳ *Paste* If you don't have (or see the need for) a garlic press, use the bottom of an unglazed, flat-bottom dish to smear a clove into a fine paste.

✳ *Chopping/mincing* To keep young, ripe garlic from sticking to the sides of your knife, sprinkle a few drops of oil on the cloves before starting—it saves time, and keeps your fingers away from the blade.

If you're sensing a lot of garlic in your near future: instead of mincing garlic each time you need it, pulse a lot of whole cloves in a food processor, refrigerate in an airtight container, and use within one week.

TOMATO TIPS

One or two tomatoes aren't hard to handle, but working with a bunch can quickly become frustrating. If you need to remove seeds and have a salad spinner, roughly chop your tomatoes and give them a few spins. Voilà! Most of the seeds will have separated from the meat. Need to peel a bunch at one time? To peel a tomato, first use your paring knife to cut out the stem. Then score a shallow X in the bottom end. Drop the tomatoes into boiling water for 15 to 30 seconds, let cool, and then peel. The skins will come right off. If you have only a few, use tongs or a fork to hold each one over a burner of a gas or electric stove until the skin just blisters, and then you can peel away. Campfire songs are welcome.

WHEN YOUR TEA KETTLE'S WHEEZY, BLANCHING IS EASY!

When a recipe calls for blanched vegetables, you end up waiting for an entire pot of water to boil just so you can dunk something in it for a few seconds (or maybe a few minutes). We all know that a watched pot never boils, so the next time a recipe calls for blanching spinach, beans, or a small amount of anything, try this quick technique. Fill a tea kettle halfway with water and set it over high heat. Put whatever needs blanching in a colander in the sink. When you hear the whistle, slowly pour the boiling water over your veggies to give them a quick cook.

SHRED IT BETTER AND SAVE SOME CHEDDAR

It's more cost effective to buy cheese in a block and shred it yourself than buy it preshredded. You can shred the whole block all at once, put the cheese in a large zip-top storage bag, and toss it in the refrigerator. You get the same effect you would if you bought the cheese already shredded, and you'll have more money in your pocket!

CASSEROLES
FOR ALL!

Favorite Classics
for the Whole Gang

What's for dinner? We bet you can't count the number of times you asked—or have been asked—this question. Well, just when you've run out of dinner ideas to satisfy the masses, the Casserole Queens swoop in to save the day! In this chapter, we've worked in a few unique twists to traditional casserole recipes and given them our stamp of approval. Enjoy tasty tried-and-true dishes such as flavorful sausages baked with fennel and feel-good potpies any night of the week. Soon you'll find yourself dubbed a dinnertime hero. No worries—you can thank us later!

- **DECONSTRUCTED CABBAGE ROLLS (AKA PIGS OUT OF THE BLANKET)**

- **BBQ PORK RIBS**

- **"LIKE A GOOD NEIGHBOR" HAM AND GRUYÈRE STRATA**

- **NEW ENGLAND POTPIE**

- **REUBEN SAMMY CASSEROLE**

- **CHICKEN WITH 40 CLOVES OF GARLIC**

- **SHRIMP GUMBO CASSEROLE**

- **MACARONI-AND-BEEF CASSEROLE**

- **BAKED SAUSAGES WITH FENNEL**

- **INDIVIDUAL BACON-WRAPPED MEATLOAVES**

DECONSTRUCTED CABBAGE ROLLS
(aka Pigs Out of the Blanket)

Even the Casserole Queens had to get their cooking career started somehow. Other than peanut butter and crackers, pigs-in-a-blanket was the first "gourmet" dish Sandy learned to prepare as a child, straight out of the 1957 edition of *Betty Crocker's Cook Book for Boys and Girls*. Those little pigs, all warm and cozy in their fancy blankets, became a weekly Saturday night staple. Then a friend of the family came to visit from up north (the big city!) and rocked Sandy's world by cooking a meal that put pigs-in-a-blanket smack on center stage as the main entrée. You can imagine Sandy's surprise when she realized that her friend's version called for ground pork to be rolled up in cabbage blankets and covered with a tomato sauce. Her friend said that this is how they are made in Poland, where her family came from. Sandy was hooked from the first delicious bite. In recent years, she's been deconstructing the recipe so that the dish is more layered, taking the pigs "out of the blanket" to become a true casserole! *Serves 8*

GLUTEN-FREE

Cooking spray

1 tablespoon olive oil

2 pounds lean ground pork

1 small onion, chopped

½ green bell pepper, chopped

1 celery rib, chopped

1 teaspoon salt

½ teaspoon freshly ground black pepper

1 (14.5-ounce) can condensed tomato soup

1 tablespoon cider vinegar

2 teaspoons minced garlic

¼ head cabbage, shredded

2 russet potatoes, peeled and thinly sliced

12 slices bacon

1 Preheat the oven to 350°F. Spray a 9 x 13-inch casserole dish with cooking spray.

2 In a large sauté pan set over medium heat, heat the olive oil. Add the pork, onion, green pepper, celery, salt, and pepper. Cook for 15 minutes, until the pork is no longer pink and the veggies are soft.

3 Meanwhile, in a medium bowl, combine the tomato soup, vinegar, and garlic.

4 Layer half of the cabbage in the prepared casserole dish, followed by half of the pork mixture, half of the potatoes, and half of the tomato sauce. Repeat the layers with the remaining ingredients. Top with the bacon.

5 Cover the dish and bake for 1½ to 2 hours, or until the sauce is bubbling and the top is browned.

BBQ PORK RIBS

The Queens have a little secret: we are slightly addicted to the thrill of competing in cook-offs. Well, at least Sandy is. Crystal just likes to dress up in costumes, decorate the camp, and mingle among the crowd all day! It's that combination of competitive spirit and social activity that makes cook-offs so unique and fun. Our particular favorite is the pride of Sandy's hometown, the Hargill Pan de Campo Cook-off. In recent years, we have taken home several trophies: second place in the Chili category, third place in Beans, and second place in Carne Guisada. But unfortunately we still haven't captured the top prize (insert *Throwdown! with Bobby Flay* flashbacks here) and, gosh darn it, we want those first-place braggin' rights! Our goal is to perfect our rib recipe this year and take the trophy home. But with Sandy living in a Washington, DC, apartment, it's hard for her to break out the smoker. Lucky for all of us, she's developed a pretty darn good recipe using just her oven. Serve with a side of Crystal's May-I-Have-More-Mayo Potato Salad (page 130), Spinach and Spice and Everything Nice (page 140), or Simple Herb-Roasted Vegetables (page 157), and you are set. Enjoy! *Serves 4*

Cooking spray

½ onion, chopped

1 celery rib, chopped

2 tablespoons packed dark brown sugar

½ teaspoon salt

¼ teaspoon paprika

2 tablespoons unsalted butter, melted

½ cup ketchup

¼ cup Heinz chili sauce

2 tablespoons cider vinegar

1 tablespoon Worcestershire sauce

Juice of 1 lemon

5 drops Tabasco

2 pounds pork ribs

1 Preheat the oven to 350°F. Spray a 9 x 13-inch casserole dish with cooking spray.

2 In a large bowl, combine the onion, celery, brown sugar, salt, paprika, butter, ketchup, chili sauce, vinegar, Worcestershire sauce, lemon juice, Tabasco, and ½ cup water.

3 Put the ribs in the prepared casserole dish and pour in the sauce, making sure to thoroughly coat the ribs. Bake, uncovered and basting every 20 to 30 minutes, for 2 to 2½ hours, until a meat thermometer registers 160°F.

This recipe is GLUTEN-FREE, as long as you make sure that the ingredients required (ketchup, Worcestershire, chili sauce) are all gluten-free brands. See page 15 for recommendations of our favorite brands.

"LIKE A GOOD NEIGHBOR"
Ham and Gruyère Strata

We are just like everyone else. We stumble in high heels, burn the occasional meal, and even lock our keys in the car. Sandy wouldn't have discovered this recipe if she hadn't locked her keys in her car the week she started her first job after college. She was heading home from work and stopped at the grocery store to grab something really quick, so she left her car running (never a good idea, no matter how cold it is!). When she returned, her doors were locked! Luckily, her new neighbor, Mrs. Dominguez, happened to be walking out to her car at the same time. She not only came to the rescue by waiting with Sandy for Pop-a-Lock to arrive but invited her over that night to eat strata. Now that's being neighborly! But something special happened as Sandy enjoyed the conversation and the amazing mushroom flavor of the meal: she totally forgot about her troubles and got lost in the moment. So if you want to meet your neighbors, invite them over and serve this dish, which is perfect for making new friends. Throw in a side of Braised Endive Gratin (page 147), and you'll be friends for life! *Serves 10*

Cooking spray

2 tablespoons olive oil

4 shallots, finely chopped

1 tablespoon unsalted butter

2 pounds fresh baby spinach

1 teaspoon fresh lemon juice

2 teaspoons salt

1 teaspoon freshly ground black pepper

6 cups (about 14 ounces) sliced cremini mushrooms

1 cup shredded deli smoked ham

¼ cup chopped fresh parsley

1 Preheat the oven to 325°F. Spray a 9 x 13-inch casserole dish with cooking spray.

2 In a large sauté pan set over medium heat, heat 1 tablespoon of the olive oil. Add half of the shallots and sauté for 2 minutes. Add the butter and cook 1 more minute. Add the spinach, lemon juice, 1 teaspoon of the salt, and ½ teaspoon of the pepper, and cook for 3 minutes, until the spinach is wilted. Spoon the spinach mixture into a large bowl and set aside. Wipe out the sauté pan with a paper towel.

3 Heat the remaining 1 tablespoon of oil in the sauté pan set over medium heat. Add the remaining shallots and sauté for 2 minutes, or until translucent. Add the mushrooms and cook for 7 minutes, until they release moisture. Remove the pan from the heat and let cool slightly. Stir in the spinach mixture, the ham, and the parsley.

8 cups cubed hearty white bread

1 cup shredded Gruyère cheese (4 ounces) (see Note)

3 cups whole milk

6 large eggs, lightly beaten

1 teaspoon dry mustard

4 Put half of the bread cubes in the bottom of the prepared casserole dish. Top with half of the mushroom mixture and ½ cup of the Gruyère. Repeat the layers with the remaining bread, mushroom mixture, and ½ cup of cheese.

5 In a small bowl, combine the milk, eggs, dry mustard, the remaining 1 teaspoon of salt, and the remaining ½ teaspoon of pepper. Pour this mixture over the layers. Cover with foil and bake for 30 minutes. Uncover and bake for 20 more minutes, until the strata is set in the middle and golden brown.

 No Gruyère? That's okay. You can easily substitute Emmentaler, Swiss, or raclette cheese.

This dish can be made GLUTEN-FREE by using your favorite gluten-free brand of bread. See page 15 for recommendations of our favorite brands.

NEW ENGLAND
Potpie

Hearty, creamy, and with a flaky crust, this potpie is straight-up comfort food. Growing up in the North Georgia mountains, Crystal mainly experienced seafood from a deep fryer. On rare occasions, her uncle Bob would travel to a fish market and bring back huge bags of fresh shrimp, which quickly lent itself to a family shrimp-eating contest. (Boy, howdy! Could Uncle Bob, her brother, Kenny, and her daddy eat some shrimp!) But it wasn't until she went to Boston for college that she really started to appreciate and love all the flavors of the sea. It didn't take long before she started experimenting with the many varieties of fresh seafood and all the ways to prepare it. One of her favorite dishes is this amazing potpie. *Serves 10*

Olive oil, for dish

2 medium russet potatoes, peeled and diced

2 teaspoons salt

6 slices bacon, chopped

1 medium onion, chopped

⅓ cup all-purpose flour

2 (8-ounce) bottles clam juice

½ cup dry white wine

¼ cup heavy cream

2 cloves garlic, finely chopped

2 teaspoons freshly ground black pepper

1 cup frozen peas and carrots, thawed

1 cup frozen corn, thawed

1 tablespoon chopped fresh thyme

1 Preheat the oven to 400°F. Lightly oil a 9 x 13-inch casserole dish.

2 Fill a large saucepan with 1 quart of water and set it over high heat. Add the potatoes and 1 teaspoon of the salt and bring to a boil, about 5 minutes. Reduce the heat to medium, cover, and simmer for 5 to 7 minutes, or until the potatoes are tender. Drain the potatoes.

3 In a separate saucepan set over medium heat, cook the bacon until crispy, about 8 minutes. Transfer to a paper towel-lined plate to drain. When cool, crumble the bacon.

4 Increase the heat to medium-high. Add the onion to the bacon drippings and cook until golden brown, about 7 minutes. Using a wire whisk, stir in the flour and cook for 1 minute to cook out the raw flour taste. Slowly stir in the clam juice, white wine, cream, garlic, the remaining teaspoon of salt, and the pepper. Cook, stirring occasionally, until thick and bubbly, 5 minutes.

¼ cup chopped fresh flat-leaf parsley

1 cup fresh shrimp (31/35), peeled, deveined, and tails removed

1 pound skinless whitefish (such as cod, hake, pollock, or haddock)

1 sheet puff pastry, thawed

5 Add the cooked potatoes, bacon, peas and carrots, corn, thyme, and parsley and stir well. Cook 3 to 4 minutes, until the mixture is hot. Stir in the shrimp and fish. Spoon the mixture into the prepared casserole dish.

6 On lightly floured surface, unfold the pastry. Roll it into a 10 x 14-inch rectangle. Using a sharp knife, cut a few slits in the pastry to allow steam to escape. Put the pastry over the hot seafood mixture and press the pastry along the edges of the casserole dish to seal.

7 Bake for 30 to 40 minutes or until the crust is deep golden brown and puffed in the center. Let stand for 10 minutes before serving.

REUBEN SAMMY
Casserole

Sandy's dad loves a good Reuben sandwich smothered in his favorite Thousand Island dressing. Without fail, every Father's Day, his wife, Margie, would make this special Reuben casserole. But Marge refused to make it on any other day of the year—not even his birthday. Even though the whole family begged for it all the time, it was considered a very special treat. Only Marge knew the way to her man's heart—straight to the belly and covered in Swiss cheese! I guess it works, because they've been married over fifty-five years! *Serves 8*

Cooking spray

16 slices rye bread, cubed

¼ cup Thousand Island dressing, homemade (page 120) or store bought

8 ounces corned beef, thinly sliced and chopped

16 ounces sauerkraut, homemade (page 201) or store bought, well drained

4 kosher dill spears, chopped

1 teaspoon caraway seeds

2 cups shredded Swiss cheese (8 ounces)

3 cups whole milk

6 large eggs

¼ cup honey mustard

1 Preheat the oven to 350°F. Spray a 9 x 13-inch casserole dish with cooking spray.

2 Line the bottom of the casserole with half of the bread cubes, cutting to fit. Spread half of the dressing over the top. Cover with half of the corned beef, half of the drained sauerkraut, half of the pickles, and half of the caraway seeds. Sprinkle with half of the cheese. Repeat the layers.

3 In a bowl, combine the milk, eggs, and mustard. Beat well and pour the mixture over the layers. Let stand on the counter for 15 minutes to let the bread fully absorb the liquid.

4 Bake for 45 minutes, or until the casserole has set and the top is golden brown. Remove the dish from the oven and let stand 10 minutes before serving.

CHICKEN WITH 40 CLOVES OF GARLIC

It's a good thing this dish will ward off vampires, because nothing ruins a dinner party like unwanted guests. If you've never had the pleasure of eating chicken with forty cloves of garlic, please don't be alarmed. What, you'd rather have vampires knocking at your door? In all seriousness, the garlic mellows as it roasts, and it takes on a slightly mild nutty flavor. And to round out your meal, this recipe works extremely well with simple sides such as our Aunt Fannie's Cabin Squash Casserole (page 148); Brussels Sprouts with Bacon, Garlic, and Shallots (page 146); or our Wild Rice (page 156). Either way, it adds a surprisingly clever twist to the standard chicken dish that some people say is "to die for." *Serves 8*

GLUTEN-FREE

DIABETIC-FRIENDLY

Cooking spray

2 medium onions, chopped

4 celery ribs, cut into ¼-inch slices

1 teaspoon dried tarragon

3 tablespoons chopped fresh parsley

8 chicken thighs, skinned (about 2¾ pounds)

8 chicken drumsticks, skinned (about 1¾ pounds)

3 tablespoons olive oil

1½ teaspoons salt

¼ teaspoon freshly ground black pepper

½ cup dry vermouth (you can use sherry or dry white wine in a pinch)

40 garlic cloves, separated but not peeled

1 Preheat the oven to 325°F. Spray a 9 x 13-inch casserole dish with cooking spray.

2 Combine the onions, celery, tarragon, and parsley in the prepared casserole dish.

3 Rub the chicken pieces with the olive oil and season with the salt and pepper. Put the chicken on top of the onions and celery. Drizzle with the vermouth and tuck the garlic in and around the chicken.

4 Cover the casserole with foil. Bake for 1½ hours, or until internal temperature of the chicken is 160°F.

SHRIMP GUMBO
Casserole

Sandy has been making this recipe for probably twenty years and has slowly perfected it over time. She knew she had finally mastered this dish when she took it to her friend's baby shower. She'd traveled up to Minneapolis, and it was freezing up there (something we Texas gals aren't used to). Sandy thought this would be the perfect thing to keep their bellies full and bodies warm. Well, she definitely picked the right recipe, because not ten minutes into the baby shower, the electricity went out and didn't come back on for about two hours. All they had was a roaring fire in the fireplace and this casserole to comfort them! Luckily, the casserole hit the spot and kept them cozy with its Creole-spiced shrimp filling and satisfying biscuit topping. *Serves 8*

3 tablespoons olive oil

1 onion, chopped

½ green bell pepper, chopped

3 celery stalks with leaves, chopped

3 garlic cloves, minced

2 (28-ounce) cans diced tomatoes

1 (15-ounce) can tomato sauce

1 tablespoon plus ½ teaspoon salt

1¼ teaspoons freshly ground black pepper

1 teaspoon chili powder

1 teaspoon dried thyme

2 bay leaves

1 pound okra, sliced

1 pound fresh shrimp (31/35), peeled and deveined

1 Preheat the oven to 450°F.

2 In a large saucepan set over medium-high heat, heat the olive oil, then add the onion, green pepper, celery, and garlic. Cook, stirring, for 6 minutes, until soft. Add the tomatoes, tomato sauce, 1 tablespoon of the salt, pepper, chili powder, thyme, and bay leaves. Cover and cook slowly for 20 minutes. Add the okra, shrimp, and the gumbo filé, and cook for 3 to 5 minutes, until the shrimp turns pink. Remove the bay leaves.

3 In a medium bowl, combine the flour, baking powder, cayenne pepper, sugar, baking soda, and the remaining ½ teaspoon of salt. Using a fork, cut in the butter until the mixture resembles coarse cornmeal. Stir in the buttermilk until the mixure just comes together. Knead until a soft dough forms.

4 On a lightly floured surface, roll out the dough until it is ½ inch thick. Using a 2½-inch round cutter, stamp out 12 biscuits.

2 teaspoons gumbo filé
(see Note)

2 cups all-purpose flour

1 tablespoon baking powder

1/2 teaspoon cayenne
pepper

2 teaspoons sugar

1/2 teaspoon baking soda

5 1/2 tablespoons cold
unsalted butter, cut into
small pieces

3/4 cup buttermilk

5 **Pour the hot gumbo into a 9 x 13-inch casserole dish. Arrange the biscuits on top of the gumbo. Bake until the biscuits are golden brown, about 20 minutes.**

Filé powder is a necessity for cooking authentic Creole or Cajun cuisine. In addition to contributing an unusual flavor, the powder also acts as a thickener when added to liquid. You can find it at most grocery stores or online at Amazon.com. We like the McCormick brand.

MACARONI-AND-BEEF
Casserole

If you're looking for something that's easy to make and tasty enough to fill those growling bellies, this is your recipe. Growing up, Crystal's family usually kept a close eye on the budget, so her mother learned how to get creative in the kitchen. One night, her mom pulled an assortment of ingredients from her pantry and fridge and created this dish from scratch. It was like magic! This casserole is, to this day, Crystal's father's favorite thing to eat. It's amazing how you can go from "nothing in the pantry" to an instant family classic. We've modified the recipe a bit, but we have a feeling it'll work wonders for your family, too. *Serves 8*

Cooking spray

1 pound elbow macaroni

2 tablespoons olive oil

2 tablespoons unsalted butter

1 onion, chopped

1 green bell pepper, chopped

2 pounds ground beef

2 teaspoons salt

1 teaspoon freshly ground black pepper

2 tablespoons all-purpose flour

1 (15-ounce) can crushed tomatoes

8 ounces sharp Cheddar cheese, shredded (2 cups)

1 cup whole milk

1/4 cup chopped fresh parsley

1/3 cup cornflakes

1 Preheat the oven to 350°F. Spray a 9 x 13-inch casserole dish with cooking spray.

2 In a large pot of boiling salted water, cook the macaroni until al dente. Drain well and transfer the macaroni to a bowl. Toss the pasta with 1 tablespoon of the olive oil.

3 In a large skillet set over medium heat, heat the remaining 1 tablespoon of olive oil and the butter. Add the onion and bell pepper and cook until softened, about 5 minutes. Add the ground beef, 1 teaspoon salt, 1/2 teaspoon pepper, and continue cooking, stirring occasionally, until the meat is browned and any liquid has evaporated, about 8 minutes.

4 Add the flour and stir well. Add the tomatoes. Bring to a simmer and cook until the sauce thickens, about 15 minutes. Add the cooked macaroni, 1 cup of the cheese, the milk, parsley, remaining 1 teaspoon salt, and remaining 1/2 teaspoon pepper. Pour the mixture into the prepared casserole dish.

5 Combine the remaining 1 cup cheese with the cornflakes and sprinkle the mixture on top of the casserole. Bake for about 20 minutes, until the casserole is bubbling and the cheese is melted. Let stand for 5 minutes.

FREEZES WELL! For best results, prepare the casserole through step 4. Wrap it with foil and freeze for up to 2 months. Thaw the casserole overnight in the refrigerator. The next day, prepare the topping and bake as stated in the recipe. Note that casseroles that have not been completely thawed may take 15 to 30 minutes longer, so be sure to check for bubbling edges and a hot center.

This dish can be made GLUTEN-FREE by using your favorite gluten-free macaroni and replacing the flour with a gluten-free mix, either store bought (see page 15 for recommendations of our favorite brands) or homemade (see page 186 for our recipe).

BAKED SAUSAGES
with Fennel

Maybe you can relate to this, too: about three or four times a year, we get one of those stop-what-you're-doing immediate cravings for Italian sausage. Maybe it's TV commercials with tantalizing close-ups, or the smell of your neighbors barbecuing, or even a flashback to that memorable sausage pizza you had in Manhattan. Either way, if it's sausage you crave, then it's sausage you shall have! Instead of just eating it straight up, we've created a recipe that turns this delicious food into a complete meal. The potatoes and tomatoes help fill you up, while the fennel bulbs and seeds add a crunch and a slightly sweet taste. Trust us, this meal is bursting with flavor, and we guarantee it will satisfy that hankering for sausage! Try serving it with our Panzanella Salad (page 134) and some crusty bread. *Serves 6*

GLUTEN-FREE

Cooking spray

2 tablespoons olive oil

1 pound spicy Italian sausages

2 tablespoons unsalted butter

1 fennel bulb, cored and thinly sliced (see Note)

3 garlic cloves, minced

1 teaspoon fennel seeds

1 pound russet potatoes (about 2), peeled and chopped

1/2 teaspoon salt

1/3 cup dry white wine

1 (28-ounce) can diced tomatoes, drained

6 ounces Gruyère cheese, grated (about 1 1/2 cups)

2 tablespoons chopped fresh parsley

1 Preheat the oven to 450°F. Spray a 9 x 13-inch casserole dish with cooking spray.

2 In a large sauté pan set over medium heat, heat 1 tablespoon of the olive oil. Add the sausages and cook, turning, until browned and cooked through, about 10 minutes. Transfer to a cutting board. When the sausages are cool enough to handle, cut them into 1/4-inch slices.

3 Add the remaining 1 tablespoon of oil and the butter to the same pan and heat over medium heat. Add the fennel bulb, garlic, and fennel seeds, cover the pan, and cook for 5 minutes. Stir in the potatoes and salt, cover the pan again, and continue cooking until the vegetables start to soften, about 5 minutes. Stir in the wine and simmer until evaporated, about 10 minutes. Stir in the tomatoes. Increase the heat to medium-high and simmer until all of the liquid has evaporated, 2 to 3 minutes. Stir in the sausages and transfer the mixture to the prepared casserole dish.

4 Bake for 10 minutes. Remove the dish from the oven and sprinkle the Gruyère over the top. Return the dish to the oven and bake until the vegetables are tender and the cheese is melted, about 10 more minutes. Allow to sit for 5 minutes and then sprinkle the top with the parsley. Serve.

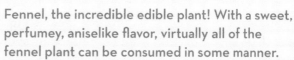

Fennel, the incredible edible plant! With a sweet, perfumey, aniselike flavor, virtually all of the fennel plant can be consumed in some manner. The roots and stalks can be cooked and eaten as a vegetable or used to add flavor to soups. The stems are a refreshing addition when chopped and added to salads, and the bulb is a welcome ingredient in baked fish or roasted vegetables. The seeds are great on pizza and are commonly used to flavor pickles, liqueurs, tomato sauces, and sausages. Even the fennel oil is used in candy and liqueurs!

INDIVIDUAL BACON-WRAPPED
Meatloaves

There are certain food pairings that never vary in the Pollock house. When meatloaf is on the table, it's a given that scalloped potatoes and green beans are faithfully by its side. The Pollocks' classic family meatloaf recipe has evolved a bit in our kitchen, as it now includes a spicy Bloody Mary mix. We also wrap each one in bacon for an elegant touch and great flavor. But we still eat it with scalloped potatoes and green beans! For a quick and easy twist on scalloped potatoes, try Mamaw's Potato Casserole (page 141). *Serves 8*

Cooking spray

12 slices bacon

1 cup ketchup

3/4 cup balsamic vinegar

2 teaspoons red pepper flakes

1/2 cup homemade Spicy Bloody Mary mix (page 203), or your favorite store-bought mix

2 large eggs, beaten

1 garlic clove, minced

3/4 cup seasoned bread crumbs, homemade (see page 188) or store bought

2 tablespoons chopped fresh parsley

1/2 teaspoon dried oregano

1/2 teaspoon salt

1/4 teaspoon freshly ground black pepper

2 pounds ground beef

8 ounces mozzarella cheese, shredded (2 cups)

1/2 cup grated Parmesan cheese (2 ounces)

1 Preheat the oven to 400°F. Spray a 9 x 13-inch casserole dish with cooking spray.

2 In a large sauté pan set over medium-high heat, cook the bacon just until lightly browned, but still soft, 6 to 8 minutes. Drain on paper towels.

3 In a large bowl, combine the ketchup, vinegar, and red pepper flakes.

4 In a separate bowl, combine the Bloody Mary mix, eggs, garlic, bread crumbs, parsley, oregano, salt, and pepper. Add the ground beef and mix well. Scoop the mixture onto a sheet of waxed paper and shape it into a 9 x 13-inch rectangle. Sprinkle the mozzarella over the top. Starting from a short side, carefully roll the meat up like a jelly roll. Cut it into 1½-inch-thick slices. Wrap the edge of each slice with two strips of the cooked bacon, overlapping as needed and securing the ends with wooden picks.

5 Pour 1 cup of the ketchup mixture into the prepared casserole dish. Put each meatloaf slice flat into the sauce. Top the casserole with ¾ cup of the ketchup sauce. Sprinkle with the Parmesan cheese and bake for 1 hour, until the sauce has thickened and the meatloaf is cooked through.

FREEZES WELL! **For best results, prepare the casserole until it's ready to put in the oven. Wrap in foil and freeze for up to 2 months. Thaw the casserole overnight in the refrigerator. Note that casseroles that have not been completely thawed may take 15 to 30 minutes longer, so be sure to check for bubbling edges and a hot center.**

This dish can be made GLUTEN-FREE by eliminating the bread crumbs and substituting oats that have been processed in a wheat-free factory. You can also purchase gluten-free bread crumbs (see page 15 for recommendations of our favorite brands) or make your own (see page 188 for our recipe).

To make this dish DIABETIC-FRIENDLY, substitute oats for the bread crumbs. Oats work well instead of bread crumbs to help bind a meatloaf, and they are high in fiber, which is important for diabetics.

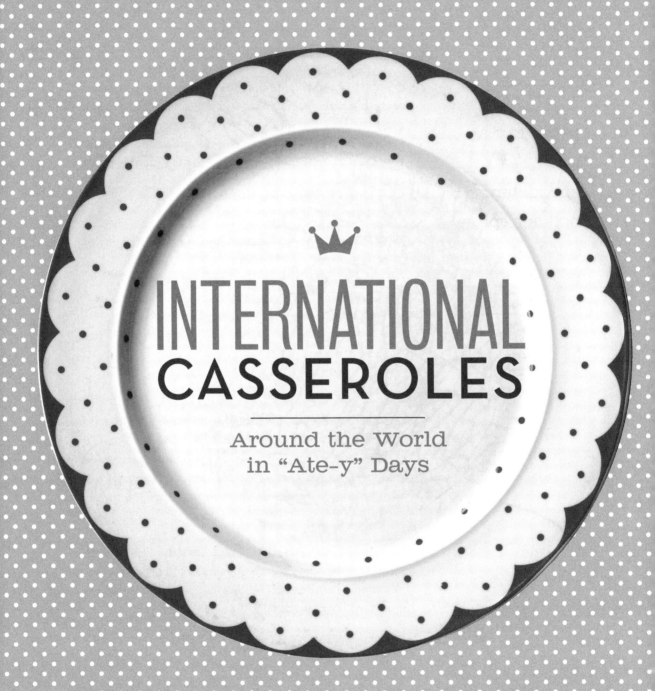

INTERNATIONAL
CASSEROLES

Around the World
in "Ate-y" Days

When you hear the words *lasagna, kugel,* and *moussaka,* do you think of casseroles? Maybe not, but take a second look. You might think you floated through childhood never encountering a casserole, when in actuality your family's holiday spread featured a pan of layered goodness. A casserole in disguise! Maybe it had an alias—an exotic name from a faraway land—but there's no denying it when you recognize its 9 × 13-inch frame. Casseroles are sneaky like that.

- MOUSSAKA

- OVEN-BAKED SPANISH TORTILLA

- YVONNE'S UNSTUFFED POBLANO CASSEROLE

- SHAKSHUKA

- BOBOTIE

- CIOPPINO-STYLE ROASTED CRAB

- THE "SITCH" CHICKEN PARMESAN

- GNOCCHI BAKE

- CHICKEN ENCHILADAS

- AWESOME AUSSIE MEAT PIES

- CHICKEN PAPRIKASH

MOUSSAKA

Moussaka always reminds Crystal and her niece Maggie of the movie *My Big Fat Greek Wedding.* If you've seen it, you may recall a scene where a grade-school-age Nia Vardalos brings moussaka to lunch, and the other girls at the table think it's called "moose caca." Well, they sure missed out, because this is a very special casserole that is perfect for Sunday dinners or potluck gatherings. And the beauty of it is that it freezes well, with no loss of flavor. We've opted to omit the traditional béchamel sauce to cut back on some of the calories, but we have included our favorite béchamel recipe if you would like to indulge. Just pour it over the top before adding the bread crumbs. What are you waiting for? Make this dish for your family, and they'll treat you like their own Greek goddess. This dish pairs nicely with our Tomato and Feta Salad (page 125). *Serves 8*

Cooking spray

3 large eggplants

1 teaspoon salt

½ teaspoon freshly ground black pepper

4 tablespoons olive oil

1 medium onion, chopped

2 garlic cloves, minced

½ lemon, cut in thin slices

¼ cup chopped fresh oregano leaves

¼ cup chopped fresh flat-leaf parsley

2 pounds ground lamb

1 cinnamon stick

3 tablespoons tomato paste

1 (15.5-ounce) can crushed tomatoes

1 cup feta cheese, crumbled (8 ounces)

1 cup freshly grated Parmesan cheese (4 ounces)

1 Preheat the oven to 350°F. Spray a 9 x 13-inch glass or ceramic casserole dish with cooking spray.

2 Cut off the stems of the eggplants and, using a vegetable peeler, peel them. Cut them lengthwise into ½-inch-thick slices. Season both sides of the pieces with ½ teaspoon of the salt and ¼ teaspoon of the pepper.

3 In a large skillet set over medium heat, heat 3 tablespoons of the oil. Working in batches, fry the eggplant in a single layer, turning once, until brown on both sides, about 8 minutes per side. Transfer the eggplant to a paper towel–lined plate to drain.

4 Add the remaining 1 tablespoon of oil to the pan and add the onion, garlic, lemon slices, oregano, and parsley. Cook, stirring, until soft, about 3 minutes. Add the lamb, cinnamon stick, the remaining ½ teaspoon of the salt, and the remaining ¼ teaspoon of the pepper, and cook until lamb is browned through. Stir in the tomato paste and crushed tomatoes. Simmer until the liquid has evaporated, stirring occasionally. Remove from the heat. Remove cinnamon stick and lemon slices.

3 cups Béchamel (recipe follows; optional)

1 cup bread crumbs (see page 188)

5 Line the bottom of the prepared casserole dish with a third of the eggplant slices; they should completely cover the bottom. Spread half of the meat sauce over the eggplant, and sprinkle half of the feta and half of the Parmesan on top. Repeat the layers again, ending with a final layer of eggplant. If using the béchamel sauce, pour it over the top. Cover with a layer of bread crumbs.

6 Bake for 30 to 40 minutes, or until the top is golden. Let cool for 10 minutes before serving.

(RECIPE CONTINUES)

FREEZES WELL! For best results, prepare the casserole (without the béchamel) through step 5. Wrap in foil and freeze for up to 2 months. Thaw the casserole overnight in the refrigerator before baking as stated in the recipe. Note that casseroles that have not been completely thawed may take 15 to 30 minutes longer, so be sure to check for bubbling edges and a hot center.

This dish can be made GLUTEN-FREE by using gluten-free bread crumbs, either store bought (see page 15 for recommendations of our favorite brands) or homemade (see page 188 for our recipe). If you want to add the béchamel to the recipe, you can make it gluten-free by eliminating the flour and substituting a gluten-free all-purpose mix, which you may purchase at most local grocery chains, or you can make your own (see page 186).

Béchamel

The moussaka recipe calls for only three cups of the bécha-mel, but you may want to serve extra on the side, too. This sauce is delicious on lots of things—especially salmon cro-quettes or vegetable lasagna.

MAKES ABOUT 6 CUPS

4 cups whole milk
½ cup (1 stick) unsalted butter
½ cup all-purpose flour
1 teaspoon salt
½ teaspoon ground nutmeg
4 large egg yolks

1 In a medium saucepan set over medium heat, heat the milk for about 10 minutes or until milk registers 160°F on a thermometer.

2 In a separate medium saucepan set over low heat, melt the butter. Slowly whisk in the flour and continue to whisk for 2 minutes.

3 Little by little, and while whisking constantly, pour in the steaming milk. It will set up and thicken dramatically at first, but as you continue adding milk, the sauce will loosen. Increase the heat to medium. Add the salt and nutmeg and stir well.

4 Put the egg yolks in a bowl and whisk well. Slowly, and while whisking constantly, pour a couple of cups of the hot béchamel into the eggs. Slowly pour the egg mixture back into the saucepan and whisk well. Keep the sauce on very low heat until ready to use; do not let simmer or boil. Per the recipe, you will use only half for this recipe, but you may serve extra on the side.

OVEN-BAKED
Spanish Tortilla

If you've ever had the chance to visit Spain, it probably left a special place in your heart. From the rustic Spanish architecture to the vibrant quality of life and the renowned cuisine, Spain truly has its own distinct flair. When Sandy and her husband, Michael, spent some time in this country, they quickly fell in love with the variety of traditional foods, eaten at all hours of the day. This classic Spanish dish goes by two names: *tortilla de patatas* or *tortilla española*. How's that for a bit of worldly knowledge? It's an excellent option for a satisfying breakfast treat, lunch, dinner, or a unique tapa at a dinner party. Serve with our Verde Sauce on page 198. Like most of our casserole recipes, it can be made ahead and lends itself to many creative variations. Our version is vegetarian, but you can always add protein, such as small bits of precooked chorizo, bacon, or sliced prosciutto. *Serves 10*

GLUTEN-FREE
VEGETARIAN!

Cooking spray

1 pound Yukon gold potatoes, diced

¼ cup olive oil

2 garlic cloves, minced

½ tablespoon red pepper flakes

4 scallions, finely chopped

1 medium red bell pepper, seeded and diced

10 large eggs

1 cup sour cream

½ cup Parmesan cheese, grated (2 ounces)

1 teaspoon salt

½ teaspoon freshly ground black pepper

1 Preheat the oven to 375°F. Spray a large cast-iron skillet or a 9 x 13-inch casserole dish with cooking spray.

2 Put the potatoes in a small saucepan and cover with cold water. Bring to a boil, reduce heat to low, and cook for 5 to 7 minutes, until the potatoes are tender. Drain and set aside to cool slightly.

3 In a large skillet set over medium heat, combine the olive oil, garlic, red pepper flakes, green onions, and bell pepper. Cook, stirring, for about 5 minutes, or until the onions are soft but not browned. Let cool slightly, then stir in the cooked potatoes.

4 In a large bowl, combine the eggs, sour cream, cheese, salt, and pepper. Stir in the vegetable-potato mixture. Pour the mixture into the prepared casserole and smooth the top.

5 Bake for 40 minutes, or until golden brown, puffed, and set in the center. Let cool for 10 minutes before serving.

YVONNE'S UNSTUFFED POBLANO
Casserole

When you think about peppers, comfort food usually isn't the first thing that comes to mind. But to Crystal and Sandy, it means home to them, and for different reasons.  Crystal's mamaw always made great stuffed peppers, and we put that recipe in our first cookbook. And when Sandy tastes a poblano pepper, she's instantly reminded of this recipe, since Sandy's oldest sister, Yvonne, makes these for her every time she comes home for a visit!

Poblano peppers are smaller and spicier than their bell pepper cousins, but they're not too hot. Fairly mild overall, they pack a ton of flavor. Best of all, they're perfect for stuffing with a variety of ingredients. We love to serve this with our Tomato and Avocado Salad (page 127). *Serves 8*

Cooking spray

4 poblano chilies, cut in half crosswise and seeded

1 pound ground beef

1/2 onion, chopped

1 teaspoon ground cumin

1 teaspoon salt

1/2 teaspoon freshly ground black pepper

3 cups shredded Monterey Jack cheese (12 ounces)

1/4 cup all-purpose flour

4 large eggs, beaten

1 1/2 cups whole milk

1/4 teaspoon Tabasco

1 Preheat the oven to Broil. Spray a 9 x 13-inch casserole dish with cooking spray.

2 Put the poblanos, skin sides up, on a foil-lined baking sheet and flatten them with your hand. Broil for 10 minutes, or until the poblanos are blackened. Put the poblanos in a plastic zip-top bag and seal. Let stand 10 minutes.

3 Decrease the oven temperature to 350°F.

4 In a large skillet set over medium-high heat, combine the beef and onion. Cook, breaking up any lumps with the back of a spoon, until the beef is browned through, about 10 minutes. Drain off the fat, and then sprinkle with the cumin, 1/2 teaspoon of the salt, and the pepper.

5 Put half of the poblanos in the prepared casserole dish. Sprinkle with the cheese and top with the meat mixture. Arrange remaining poblanos over the meat.

6 Mix the flour and the remaining ½ teaspoon of the salt in a bowl. In a separate bowl, combine the beaten eggs, milk, and Tabasco. Gradually add the egg mixture to the flour and stir until smooth. Pour over the casserole.

7 Bake for 45 to 50 minutes, or until a knife inserted just off-center comes out clean. Let cool for 5 to 10 minutes before serving.

FREEZES WELL! For best results, prepare the casserole through step 6. Wrap in foil and freeze for up to 2 months. Thaw the casserole overnight in the refrigerator before baking as stated in the recipe. Note that casseroles that have not been completely thawed may take 15 to 30 minutes longer, so be sure to check for bubbling edges and a hot center.

This dish can be made GLUTEN-FREE by replacing the flour with a gluten-free all-purpose mix, either store bought (see page 15 for recommendations of our favorite brands) or homemade (see page 186 for our recipe).

SHAKSHUKA

Just imagine how worldly you will appear the next time you have houseguests and you say you are going to have bobotie (pronounced "buh-*boor*-tea") (see page 62) for dinner and shakshuka the following day for brunch. Equally impressive and equally as fun to say! Bobotie, shakshuka . . .

GLUTEN-FREE

DIABETIC-FRIENDLY

VEGETARIAN!

Shakshuka is a wildly popular and easy-to-make Israeli dish made with eggs (see, feels like home already!) poached in a flavorful sauce usually consisting of tomatoes, chili peppers, and onions, often spiced with cumin. Aside from the great taste, there are many reasons to love this recipe. It is naturally vegetarian, gluten-free, and diabetic-friendly, and it's very easy to make and/or adapt! Shakshuka is like that flexible friend who can go with you anywhere and fit in perfectly, no matter the crowd. Since it's egg based, you can serve it for breakfast, lunch, or dinner, but the Israelis usually eat it for breakfast. We love to serve it with some whole-wheat pita bread (to soak up all the delicious sauce!) for a light evening meal. *Serves 6*

Cooking spray

¼ cup olive oil

2 jalapeño peppers, stemmed, seeded, and finely chopped

3 shallots, chopped

5 garlic cloves, crushed and sliced

2 teaspoons smoked paprika

1 teaspoon ground cumin

1 teaspoon salt

½ teaspoon cayenne pepper

1 (28-ounce) can crushed tomatoes

1 Preheat the oven to 350°F. Spray a 9 x 13-inch casserole dish with cooking spray.

2 In a large sauté pan set over medium heat, heat the oil. Add the jalapeños and shallots and cook, stirring occasionally, until soft and golden brown, about 6 minutes. Add the garlic, paprika, cumin, salt, and cayenne. Cook, stirring frequently, until the garlic is soft, about 2 more minutes. Add the crushed tomatoes, tomato sauce, and vegetable broth. Stir well. Pour the sauce into the prepared casserole dish, cover it with foil, and put it in the oven. Bake for 20 minutes, stirring midway through.

1 (8-ounce) can tomato sauce

1/2 cup vegetable stock, homemade (see page 194) or store bought

8 large eggs

1/2 cup crumbled feta cheese (4 ounces)

1 tablespoon chopped flat-leaf parsley

6 pita bread rounds, for serving

3 Pull the casserole dish out of the oven and crack the eggs over the sauce so that the eggs are evenly distributed throughout the casserole dish. Cover the dish with foil and cook until the yolks are just set, about 10 minutes. Sprinkle with the feta and parsley and serve with the pita bread.

As we mentioned in the headnote, this dish can easily be adapted to use whatever ingredients you have on hand or for taste. Don't have shallots? Simply substitute an onion. Want to incorporate an Indian flair? Keep the cumin, replace the other spices with garam masala, and switch out the feta with goat cheese or paneer. Want to give the tomato sauce an Italian twist? Substitute roasted red bell peppers for the jalapeños and switch out the spices with oregano and basil. Yum!

BOBOTIE

Who would have thought that the national dish of South Africa is—you guessed it—a casserole! Similar to the shepherd's pie of Great Britain or Greece's moussaka, bobotie is an all-in-one meal consisting of meat with a rich egg topping. Plus it happens to be fun to say (pronounced "buh-*boor*-tea").

If you're a little sheepish about eating lamb, trust us, this is the way to go for your first try. You can make this dish with beef, too, but the bites of tender lamb mixed with the sweetness of apricots, apple, and raisins are really delicious. *Serves 8*

Cooking spray

2 thick slices white bread, torn into small pieces

¾ cup milk

¼ cup (½ stick) unsalted butter

1 large onion, finely chopped

½ pound ground lamb or beef

½ pound ground pork

1 cup slivered almonds, toasted

1 Granny Smith apple, peeled, cored, and diced

⅓ cup golden raisins

1 cup chopped dried apricots

2 tablespoons apricot jam

Juice of 1 lemon

1 tablespoon curry powder

⅛ teaspoon dried oregano

1 teaspoon salt

½ teaspoon freshly ground black pepper

1 large egg

6 lemon leaves, for garnish (see Note)

1 Preheat the oven to 325°F. Spray a 9 x 13-inch casserole dish with cooking spray.

2 In a small bowl, combine the bread and ¼ cup of the milk, and let soak for 5 minutes.

3 In a large sauté pan set over medium-high heat, melt 2 tablespoons of the butter. Add the onion and cook until it starts to soften, about 3 minutes. Add the lamb and pork and cook for 3 more minutes. Add the soaked bread, almonds, apple, raisins, apricots, jam, lemon juice, curry powder, oregano, salt, and pepper. Cook for 5 minutes. Pour the mixture into the prepared casserole dish.

4 In a small bowl, whisk together the remaining ½ cup milk and the egg. Pour half of this mixture over the meat. Dot with the remaining 2 tablespoons butter. Bake for 30 minutes. Add the remaining milk mixture and bake 5 more minutes or until set. Garnish with lemon leaves before serving.

This South African specialty is often adorned with a lemon leaf garnish. Lemon leaves can often be found at a florist. You can substitute with orange or bay leaves. If you opt for bay leaves, grate a bit of the lemon zest into the dish before adding the lemon juice (at step 3).

CIOPPINO-STYLE
Roasted Crab

We're about to tell you a crabby tale—a colorful story of how this dish originated. It all started with an Italian-American fisherman who gathered the crew's leftover catch  after a day at sea. At the end of the day, he'd throw his assortment of fish and seafood into a communal pot for supper. All the fishermen would shout in broken English, "Chip in!" to one person and "You, chip in!" to another. Over time, this is how the name *cioppino* came to be.

However it originated, most people won't deny themselves a crab-infused recipe, especially if it's baked in a warm, delicious casserole. This Italian twist is a hit for many reasons, but we think it has something to do with the dry white wine. Not only does it bring out the flavor of the crab, but we made sure the recipe calls for just enough wine for there to be a bit left over for the chef to enjoy. Plus, when it's time to clean up after dinner, you can try this "chip in!" tactic on your family. *Serves 10*

Cooking spray

¼ cup extra-virgin olive oil

1 medium onion, finely chopped

6 large garlic cloves, minced

2 cups bottled clam juice

1 cup dry white wine

2 (15-ounce) cans diced tomatoes

½ cup flat-leaf parsley leaves

1 teaspoon salt

½ teaspoon freshly ground black pepper

1 teaspoon red pepper flakes

2 bay leaves

2 (2-pound) cooked Dungeness crabs or Alaska king crab legs, cleaned, quartered, and cracked

1 Preheat the oven to 400°F. Spray a 9 x 13-inch casserole dish with cooking spray.

2 Heat the oil in a large sauté pan set over medium heat. Add the onion and garlic and sauté until soft, about 5 minutes. Add 1 cup of water, the clam juice, wine, tomatoes, parsley, salt, black pepper, red pepper, and bay leaves. Increase the heat to high and bring to a boil, 5 minutes. Reduce the heat to medium and simmer for 10 minutes. Add the crabmeat and pour the mixture into the prepared casserole dish.

3 Bake for 15 to 20 minutes, until the crab pieces are heated through. Remove the bay leaves before serving.

THE "SITCH" CHICKEN
Parmesan

Anyone who knows Crystal is well aware that she is a funny, funny girl. She finds herself in the craziest situations—like randomly standing beside "the Situation" on a little reality show called *Jersey Shore* that's based on a group of Italian Americans. Her cameo lasted a split second, but, nonetheless, it's a crazy story and we have a freeze-framed video clip to prove it. So what in the world does this have to do with our recipe? One of the characters on the show makes chicken Parmesan for a Sunday night, family-style dinner.

But let's go beyond the shores of Jersey and over to Italy. This dish is actually claimed by both Campania and Sicily and is based on *melanzane alla parmigiana*, or eggplant parmigiana, a classic southern Italian recipe. The addition of fresh basil and parsley really heightens the flavors. Pair it with a simple green salad tossed in our Lemon Parmesan Dressing (page 117) and your favorite bread. *Serves 10*

Cooking spray

½ cup vegetable oil

2 large eggs, lightly beaten

1 teaspoon salt

½ teaspoon freshly ground black pepper

1 cup bread crumbs (see page 188)

4 whole boneless, skinless, split chicken breasts

2 (15-ounce) cans tomato sauce

2 tablespoons chopped fresh parsley

¼ cup chopped fresh basil

½ teaspoon chopped fresh oregano

½ teaspoon garlic powder

2 tablespoons unsalted butter

1 Preheat the oven to 350°F. Spray a 9 x 13-inch casserole dish with cooking spray.

2 Heat the oil in a large sauté pan set over medium-high heat.

3 In a shallow dish, combine the eggs, salt, and pepper. Put the bread crumbs in a second shallow dish. Dip the chicken breasts in the egg mixture, then in the bread crumbs. Put the breaded chicken in the hot oil and cook until golden brown on both sides, about 6 minutes per side. Transfer the chicken to the prepared casserole dish.

4 In a medium saucepan set over high heat, combine the tomato sauce, 1 tablespoon of the parsley, basil, oregano, and garlic powder. Bring the sauce to a boil, reduce the heat to medium, and simmer for 10 minutes. Add the butter and when the butter has melted, pour the sauce over the chicken in the casserole dish. Sprinkle with the Parmesan cheese.

1 cup grated Parmesan cheese (4 ounces)

8 ounces mozzarella cheese, shredded (2 cups)

5 Cover the dish and bake for 30 minutes. Uncover the dish, sprinkle the mozzarella cheese on top, and bake 10 more minutes. Remove the pan from the oven, sprinkle the remaining 1 tablespoon parsley over the top of the casserole, and serve.

FREEZES WELL! For best results, prepare the casserole through step 4. Wrap in foil and freeze for up to 2 months. Thaw the casserole overnight in the refrigerator before baking as stated in the recipe. Note that casseroles that have not been completely thawed may take 15 to 30 minutes longer, so be sure to check for bubbling edges and a hot center.

This dish can be made GLUTEN-FREE by using gluten-free bread crumbs, either store bought (see page 15 for recommendations of our favorite brands) or homemade (see page 188 for our recipe).

GNOCCHI BAKE

Over in Italy, you'll find wonderfully light dumplings called gnocchi. Really easy to prepare, they're a simple combination of cooked potatoes and flour formed into little bite-size pieces. The Queens take this amazing dumpling and combine it with other traditional Italian ingredients in our trusty 9 x 13-inch dish **VEGETARIAN!** to make a gnocchi bake—our own casserole twist on a classic favorite. Ciao! If you're intimidated by the idea of making homemade gnocchi, you can find them frozen or vacuum sealed at most grocery stores. Look for a 16-ounce package for an easy substitution. Pair this dish with our Pint-Size Caprese Salad (page 126) or our Spinach and Spice and Everything Nice (page 140), and you'll have quite an Italian feast! *Serves 8*

1 pound russet potatoes, peeled and chopped

1 large egg

1 large egg yolk

1/2 cup grated Parmesan cheese (2 ounces)

1 cup all-purpose flour, plus more for dusting

2 teaspoons salt

1/2 teaspoon freshly ground black pepper

Cooking spray

1 tablespoon olive oil

1 medium onion, chopped

1 red bell pepper, seeded and finely chopped

2 garlic cloves, minced

1 (15-ounce) can diced tomatoes

1/2 cup fresh basil leaves, torn

1½ cups shredded mozzarella cheese (6 ounces)

1 Put the potatoes in a large pot and add enough water to cover them by an inch. Bring to a boil, reduce the heat to medium, and simmer until the potatoes are tender, 25 to 30 minutes. Drain and set the potatoes aside to cool slightly. When the potatoes are cool enough to handle, pass them through a ricer into a large bowl. If you don't have a ricer, you can grate the potatoes using a fine grater.

2 In a small bowl, whisk together the egg and egg yolk. Add the egg mixture, the Parmesan, flour, 1 teaspoon of the salt, and 1/4 teaspoon of the pepper to the potatoes. Using your hands, gently mix the ingredients to form a soft but not sticky dough. Transfer the dough to a floured surface. Gather into a ball, and then divide it into 4 pieces.

3 Line a rimmed baking sheet with parchment paper and dust it with flour. Working with 1 piece of dough at a time (keep the other pieces covered with a damp kitchen towel), roll the dough into a 24-inch-long rope. Cut crosswise into 1-inch pieces. Working with 1 piece at a time, press lightly on the gnocchi with the back of the tines of a fork and gently roll the gnocchi to create ridges on one side (see Note). Put the gnocchi on the prepared baking sheet and dust lightly with flour. Repeat with the remaining dough.

4 Preheat the oven to 350°F. Spray a 9 x 13-inch casserole dish with cooking spray.

5 Heat the oil in a large frying pan set over medium-high heat. Add the onion and red bell pepper and cook for 5 minutes, until soft. Stir in the garlic and fry for 1 minute. Add the tomatoes, gnocchi, the remaining 1 teaspoon of salt, and the remaining ¼ teaspoon of the pepper, and simmer for 10 to 15 minutes, stirring occasionally, until the gnocchi are soft and the sauce has thickened. Stir in the basil and pour the mixture into the prepared casserole dish. Sprinkle the casserole with the mozzarella cheese.

6 Bake for 15 to 20 minutes, until the cheese is bubbling and golden.

Did you know that the ridges on gnocchi aren't just for decoration? They actually make it easier for the sauce to cling to the dumplings. Those Italians think of everything!

CHICKEN
Enchiladas

Sandy grew up in the "Valley" and her favorite school lunch at Edinburg High School (go Bobcats!) was chicken enchilada day! And if anybody is going to make enchiladas the right way, they're probably going to do it in the Valley. If you aren't aware, the Valley is deep in the southern part of Texas near the Mexican border, and it's known for delicious Mexican-influenced dishes. As with most of our childhood favorites, we have altered the recipe ever so slightly to fit our current palates. In other words, we can handle the heat! Here is Sandy's latest and greatest. She likes to serve it up with Nene's Spanish Rice (page 153). *Serves 6*

Cooking spray

1 cup plus 2 tablespoons canola oil

3 tablespoons chili powder

2 tablespoons all-purpose flour

1/2 teaspoon ground cumin

1 cup tomato sauce

2 cups chicken stock, homemade (see page 192) or store bought

5 cups shredded Monterey Jack cheese (20 ounces)

1 medium onion, finely chopped

3 cloves garlic, minced

18 corn tortillas

1 (3-pound) roasted chicken, boned and shredded (see page 200 for our recipe)

1 Preheat the oven to 350°F. Spray a 9 x 13-inch casserole dish with cooking spray.

2 In a medium saucepan set over medium heat, heat 2 tablespoons of the oil. When the oil is hot, stir in the chili powder, flour, and cumin, and cook for 1 minute. Add the tomato sauce and chicken broth, bring to a simmer, and cook for 15 to 20 minutes, or until the sauce starts to thicken. Pour 1 cup of the sauce into the bottom of the prepared casserole dish.

3 In a medium bowl, combine the cheese, onion, and garlic. Mix well and set aside.

4 In a medium sauté pan set over medium heat, heat the remaining 1 cup of oil until hot. Turn off the heat, then, using tongs, dip each corn tortilla in the hot oil for 5 to 10 seconds to warm the tortilla and make it pliable, not crispy. Lay each hot tortilla on a paper towel–lined baking sheet to drain while you heat the remaining tortillas.

5 Take each tortilla, dip it in the sauce in the saucepan, and put it on a cutting board. Spoon ¼ cup of the cheese mixture onto the center of the tortilla and top it with roasted chicken. Roll the tortilla into an enchilada and put it seam side down in the casserole dish. Repeat with the remaining tortillas, cheese mixture (reserve 1 cup for top), and chicken. Top with the remaining sauce and reserved cheese.

6 Bake for 20 to 30 minutes, or until the cheese is bubbling and slightly brown. Let cool for 10 minutes before serving.

FREEZES WELL! For best results, prepare the casserole through step 5. Wrap in foil and freeze for up to 2 months. Thaw the casserole overnight in the refrigerator before baking as stated in the recipe. Note that casseroles that have not been completely thawed may take 15 to 30 minutes longer, so be sure to check for bubbling edges and a hot center.

This dish can be made GLUTEN-FREE by replacing the flour with a gluten-free all-purpose mix, either store bought (see page 15 for recommendations of our favorite brands) or homemade (see page 186 for our recipe).

AWESOME AUSSIE
Meat Pies

Wouldn't you know it? The national dish of Australia is also a casserole! Rob Swander, a culinary grad and our dear friend's brother, perfected this traditional dish while traveling in the wilds of the outback. Well, not quite, but he did travel all over Australia, sampling countless variations of this dish (along with all of the local brews). He spent some time in our kitchen, as an honorary Casserole King, and passed along this little taste of "down under." So this is the real deal and the perfect dish for your mates. Get your veggies in by accompanying this dish with our Simple Herb-Roasted Vegetables (page 157). *Serves 6*

DIABETIC-FRIENDLY

Cooking spray

3 tablespoons all-purpose flour

1/2 tablespoon ground cumin

1 teaspoon coriander

1/2 tablespoon salt

1 teaspoon freshly ground black pepper

2 pounds beef chuck roast, cut into 1/4-inch cubes

1/2 tablespoon unsalted butter

1 tablespoon vegetable oil

1 onion, chopped

2 garlic cloves, minced

1/3 cup soy sauce

1/3 cup Worcestershire sauce

1/2 cup Shiner beer (we love a good Texas beer!), or any strong lager

1 Preheat the oven to 350°F. Spray 6 (6-ounce) ramekins with cooking spray.

2 In a large bowl, whisk together the flour, cumin, coriander, salt, and pepper. Add the beef and toss to coat well.

3 Heat a stockpot over medium heat. Add the butter and oil. Shake any excess flour from the beef and add the beef to the pot. Cook, turning to brown all sides, for 8 to 10 minutes. Transfer the beef to a paper towel–lined plate.

4 Add the onion to the pot and cook, stirring, until it has caramelized, 10 minutes. Add the garlic and cook for about 1 minute, then quickly add the beef back to the pot, followed by the soy sauce, Worcestershire sauce, and beer. Cook for about 3 minutes and add the beef stock. Reduce the heat to medium, so that you have a low simmer, and cover the pot. Cook until the sauce has become thick like gravy, about 45 minutes to 1 hour. Divide the beef mixture among the prepared ramekins.

2 cups beef stock, homemade (page 193) or store bought

1 sheet frozen puff pastry, thawed

5 Put the puff pastry on a floured work surface. Using a rolling pin, roll it out enough to get six 4-inch circles to cover the top of the ramekins. Dust with flour if the pastry is sticky. Lay the puff pastry over the meat filling in the ramekins. Press the pastry that hangs over the side onto the edges of the dish to seal, and cut a slit in each pie.

6 Bake for 45 minutes, or until the pies are golden and crispy looking on top.

FREEZES WELL! For best results, prepare the meat pies through step 4. Wrap in foil and freeze for up to 2 months. Thaw the pies overnight in the refrigerator. The next day, top them with the pastry and bake as stated in the recipe. Note that casseroles that have not been completely thawed may take 15 to 30 minutes longer, so be sure to check for bubbling edges and a hot center.

 To eat the Aussie way, serve with tomato sauce (ketchup to you Yankees).

CHICKEN
Paprikash

Hungarian cuisine is as colorful as its culture. Chicken Paprikash is a classic Hungarian comfort food that's heavily seasoned with paprika and served over egg noodles. While we Americans are familiar with paprika the spice—a bright red powder that is either hot or sweet—in Hungary, this word really means "pepper." But don't go thinking this dish is superspicy, because ours is made with sweet paprika and has a rich, deep flavor. *Serves 6*

4 cups dried egg noodles
(2/3 of a 12-ounce bag)

6 slices bacon, chopped

1 large onion, chopped

2 large carrots, chopped

2 celery ribs, chopped

1/2 teaspoon julienned
lemon zest

2 tablespoons sweet
paprika

1 1/2 teaspoons salt

1/2 teaspoon freshly ground
black pepper

1 (8-ounce) container sour
cream

1/3 cup all-purpose flour,
sifted

1 3/4 cups whole milk

6 boneless, skinless
chicken breast halves
(2 to 2 1/4 pounds)

1 Preheat the oven to 375°F.

2 Cook the noodles according to the package directions. Drain and set aside.

3 In a large saucepan set over medium heat, cook the bacon until crisp, about 10 minutes, and set it on paper towels to drain. Into the same skillet, put the onion, carrots, and celery, and cook over medium heat for 5 minutes, or until veggies start to become brown. Stir in the lemon zest, 1 tablespoon of the paprika, 1 teaspoon of the salt, and 1/4 teaspoon of the black pepper.

4 Meanwhile, in a medium bowl, whisk together the sour cream and flour. Gradually whisk in the milk. Pour the milk mixture into the saucepan with the veggies. Cook, stirring, until the mixture is bubbly, 6 to 8 minutes. Stir in the cooked noodles and bacon.

5 Spoon the mixture into a 9 x 13-inch casserole dish. Arrange the chicken on top and sprinkle the chicken with the remaining 1/2 teaspoon salt, 1/4 teaspoon pepper, and 1 tablespoon paprika.

6 Bake for 35 to 40 minutes, or until the chicken is no longer pink inside.

FREEZES WELL! For best results, prepare the casserole through step 5. Wrap in foil and freeze for up to 2 months. Thaw the casserole overnight in the refrigerator before baking as stated in the recipe. Note that casseroles that have not been completely thawed may take an additional 15 to 30 minutes longer, so be sure to check for bubbling edges and a hot center.

This dish can be made GLUTEN-FREE by replacing the flour with a gluten-free all-purpose mix, either store-bought or homemade (see page 186) for our recipe). You will also want to use gluten-free noodles. See page 15 for recommendations of our favorite brands.

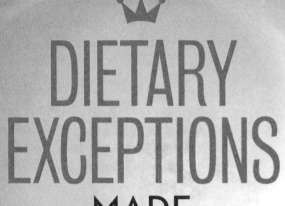

DIETARY EXCEPTIONS

MADE EXCEPTIONALLY WELL

Casseroles That
Suit Your Life!

If you suffer from a food allergy or intolerance or have made the decision to restrict your diet for whatever reason, you may feel that creating a meal is simply about making sacrifices. Think again! It can be an exciting opportunity to learn, try something new, and be creative. Try not to see it as making exceptions to your food, but as making your food exceptionally well. That's the process we adopted when developing the recipes in this chapter. From vegetarian, to gluten-free, and the diabetic-friendly, we feel confident that these are dishes the entire family will enjoy.

- **ZUCCHINI LASAGNA**

- **ROSEMARY BAKED HAM**

- **ORZO WITH ZUCCHINI, TOMATOES, AND GOAT CHEESE**

- **SUMMERTIME TOMATO BASIL PIE**

- **MERRY MUSHROOM BREAD PUDDING**

- **CHEESY GRITS-STUFFED EGGPLANT ROLLS WITH TOMATO SAUCE**

- **RUSTIC POLENTA CASSEROLE**

- **ERIN'S SPECIAL GLUTEN-FREE CORN DOG CASSEROLE**

- **SPINACH AND GRUYÈRE SOUFFLÉ**

- **THE GREAT PUMPKIN PASTA**

- **THE NELLY FRITTATA**

- **BUTTERNUT SQUASH GRATIN WITH ASIAGO CHEESE AND TOASTED PINE NUTS**

- **SHEPHERDLESS PIE**

- **FARRO, WILD MUSHROOM, AND WALNUT CASSEROLE**

- **GREEN CHILI AND CHICKEN BAKE**

ZUCCHINI LASAGNA

GLUTEN-FREE

DIABETIC-FRIENDLY

Citizens of Casseroleville, bow in the presence of the king of all baked dishes! This recipe gets two thumbs-up not only for being gluten-free, but also for allowing you to keep your blood sugar in check. By replacing lasagna noodles with thin layers of sliced zucchini, the carbs stay low, but the flavor is still full and zesty. We suggest using a mandoline for even slices and quick prep. Just be careful—those things are sharp! *Serves 8*

2½ tablespoons extra-virgin olive oil

1 small onion, finely chopped

½ teaspoon red pepper flakes

1 pound ground turkey

1 (28-ounce) can diced tomatoes

3 tablespoons chopped fresh oregano

2 teaspoons salt

2 medium zucchini

1 cup part-skim ricotta cheese

¼ teaspoon freshly ground black pepper

½ cup freshly grated Parmesan cheese (2 ounces)

1 Preheat the oven to 375°F.

2 In a large straight-sided skillet set over medium heat, heat 2 tablespoons of the oil. Add the onion and red pepper flakes and cook, stirring occasionally, until the onion is tender, about 8 minutes. Add the turkey and cook, breaking up any large pieces with the back of a spoon, until brown throughout, 3 to 4 minutes. Add the tomatoes and bring the mixture to a boil. Reduce the heat to medium and simmer until it thickens, about 20 minutes. Stir in the oregano and salt. Let cool.

3 Slice the zucchini lengthwise into thin strips (about ⅛ inch thick). Put 5 or 6 zucchini slices, overlapping slightly, in the bottom of an 8 x 8-inch baking dish. Top with 1 cup of the sauce. Dot with ¼ cup of the ricotta. Repeat the layers twice, alternating the direction of the zucchini. Top with the remaining zucchini and brush the top with the remaining ¼ teaspoon oil. Dot with the remaining ¼ cup ricotta and season with the black pepper. Top with the Parmesan cheese.

4 Bake for 50 to 60 minutes, until the lasagna is bubbling and the top is brown. Let stand for 10 minutes before serving.

FREEZES WELL! **For best results, prepare the casserole through step 3. Wrap in foil and freeze for up to 2 months. Thaw the casserole overnight in the refrigerator before baking as stated in the recipe. Note that casseroles that have not been completely thawed may take an additional 15 to 30 minutes longer, so be sure to check for bubbling edges and a hot center.**

Make this dish VEGETARIAN by simply omitting the turkey from the sauce or replacing it with ground meat substitute. We prefer MorningStar Farms Meal Starters Grillers Recipe Crumbles for use in sauces such as this.

ROSEMARY
Baked Ham

A pig walks into a bar and orders a martini . . . Okay, this isn't the beginning of a horrible joke—it's a recipe for a delicious gluten-free ham sweetened with agave, rosemary,  and sweet vermouth. You may wonder why you would need a recipe for a gluten-free ham, but prepared hams are often covered in a sweet glaze that usually contains wheat. Instead of second-guessing whether the glaze contains secret foes, we suggest making your own ham at home! The vermouth and agave add the sweet flavor you want, with no worries of hidden gluten. *Serves 16*

2 cups sweet vermouth

2 tablespoons agave nectar

1 (6-pound) fully cooked ham half

Cooking spray

3 tablespoons chopped fresh rosemary

1 teaspoon freshly ground black pepper

5 garlic cloves, minced

1 Preheat the oven to 350°F.

2 In a small heavy saucepan set over high heat, bring the vermouth and agave nectar to a boil. Boil for 15 minutes or until the mixture is reduced to about ¾ cup. Remove the pan from the heat.

3 Trim the fat and rind from the ham. Score the outside of the ham in a diamond pattern. Put the ham on a broiler pan that's been coated with cooking spray. Rub the ham all over with the rosemary, pepper, and garlic.

4 Bake for 1 hour and 30 minutes, and then brush the ham with ¼ cup of the vermouth mixture and loosely cover it with foil. Continuing to baste the ham with the vermouth mixture every 15 minutes, bake for 45 minutes more, or until a thermometer inserted in the center of the ham registers 135°F. Transfer the ham to a serving platter and let stand for 30 minutes before slicing.

ORZO with Zucchini, Tomatoes, and Goat Cheese

Summers may be hot in Texas, but that doesn't make our parties any less sizzling! We just lighten up the dishes and keep the cold drinks a-flowin'. This light yet mighty and flavorful dish is perfect for those summer backyard barbecues. It's wonderful at room temperature or served cold, so it's easy to make it the day before and spend time having summer fun with your guests instead of in the kitchen. *Serves 6*

VEGETARIAN!

1 (16-ounce) package orzo

1 tablespoon olive oil

2 medium zucchini, quartered lengthwise and thinly sliced

1 garlic clove, minced

1 (14.5-ounce) can diced tomatoes with garlic and oregano, drained

1 (7-ounce) jar roasted red bell peppers, drained and chopped

¼ cup chopped fresh parsley

1 teaspoon chopped fresh oregano

½ teaspoon salt

¼ teaspoon freshly ground black pepper

½ cup freshly grated Parmesan cheese (2 ounces)

½ cup crumbled goat cheese (2 ounces)

1 Prepare the orzo according to the package directions, omitting any salt and fat. Drain, and toss with 2 teaspoons of the olive oil.

2 Heat the remaining 1 teaspoon of oil in a large sauté pan set over medium heat. Add the zucchini and cook, stirring, for 7 minutes. Add the garlic and cook, stirring, for 3 minutes. Add the tomatoes, roasted red peppers, parsley, oregano, salt, and pepper. Cook for 5 minutes or until thoroughly heated. Remove the pan from the heat and stir in the orzo. If you plan to serve the dish hot, stir in the Parmesan and the goat cheese now. If serving it chilled, refrigerate the dish for at least 2 hours and toss with the cheese before serving.

This dish can be made GLUTEN-FREE by substituting quinoa for the orzo.

SUMMERTIME TOMATO BASIL PIE

Celebrate the bounty of summer by combining two of life's most simple but divine plea-
sures: fresh tomatoes and basil. There is little out there in food that excites Crystal more
than these ingredients, and one of her favorite things is to put them in a
VEGETARIAN! savory pie. For this recipe we recommend beefsteak tomatoes, as they
are widely available, but if you are able to find a glorious selection of heirloom tomatoes at
your local farmers' market, go ahead and substitute! *Serves 6*

1 pie crust, homemade
(page 187) or store bought

4 large beefsteak tomatoes,
peeled and thickly sliced

1½ teaspoons salt

¼ cup fresh basil leaves,
chopped, plus more for
garnish

3 green onions, green
parts, chopped

¼ teaspoon freshly ground
black pepper

½ cup Greek yogurt

¼ cup crumbled goat
cheese (1 ounce)

1 Preheat the oven to 350°F.

2 Line a 9 x 13-inch casserole dish up to the rim with the
pie dough (if homemade, use 1 recipe; if store bought, use
both pie crusts and overlap to ensure total coverage). Bake
for 15 minutes, or until golden brown. Set aside to cool.

3 Put the tomato slices in a colander in the sink in one
layer. Sprinkle them with 1 teaspoon of the salt and let
drain for 10 minutes. Next, press the tomatoes between
layers of paper towels to squeeze out more juice, and then
cut them into large pieces and put them in a large bowl.
Add the basil and onions and mix well. Season with the
remaining ½ teaspoon of salt and the pepper.

4 In a separate bowl, combine the yogurt and goat cheese.

5 Put the tomato mixture into the cooled pie shell and
spread the yogurt mixture on top. Bake for 30 minutes, or
until lightly browned. Let cool for at least 15 minutes.

6 Cut the pie into slices and serve warm with a sprinkling
of basil.

This recipe can be made GLUTEN-FREE by using a purchased
gluten-free pie crust or by making your own (see page 187
for our recipe).

MERRY MUSHROOM
Bread Pudding

The Queens have an impressive selection of vintage casserole dishes—from Pyrex to Fire King, and a whole lot of everything in between. One of our favorites happens  to be a CorningWare dish with the "Merry Mushroom" pattern on it. The orange, yellow, and brown color palette screams '70s, and we love it! We're constantly creating new mushroom recipes and proudly serving them up in this dish. Trust us, nothing perks up a buffet table like a "Merry Mushroom" painted casserole dish! This particular bread pudding is one of our finest mushroom masterpieces. The combination of portobello and button mushrooms makes it especially earthy and supercomforting. *Serves 6*

Cooking spray

3 cups whole milk

8 cups rustic bread, cut into 2-inch cubes

2 (4-ounce) portobello mushrooms

2 teaspoons vegetable oil

6 cups quartered button mushrooms (about 12 ounces)

2 garlic cloves, minced

1/2 cup chopped fresh parsley

2 teaspoons chopped fresh rosemary

1/4 teaspoon salt

1/4 teaspoon freshly ground black pepper

3 large eggs

1 large egg white

1 cup shredded Gruyère cheese (4 ounces)

1 Preheat the oven to 375°F. Spray a 9 x 13-inch casserole dish with cooking spray.

2 In a medium bowl, combine 2 cups of the milk and the bread. Cover and chill for 30 minutes, stirring occasionally.

3 Meanwhile, using a spoon, remove the brown gills from the undersides of the portobellos and remove the stems; discard the gills and stems; slice mushrooms. Heat the oil in a large nonstick skillet set over medium-high heat. Add the portobello and button mushrooms and sauté for 4 minutes, until the mushrooms start to release their juices. Stir in the garlic, parsley, rosemary, salt, and pepper, and cook for 1 minute.

4 In a medium bowl, whisk together the remaining 1 cup of milk, the eggs, and the egg white. Spoon 2 cups of the bread mixture into the prepared casserole dish. Top with the mushroom mixture and sprinkle with 1/3 cup of the cheese. Top with the remaining bread mixture and the remaining 2/3 cup cheese. Pour the egg mixture over the top. Bake for 45 minutes, or until set. Let cool 5 minutes before serving.

CHEESY GRITS-STUFFED
Eggplant Rolls with Tomato Sauce

After the fun time we had on *Throwdown! with Bobby Flay*, we were asked to shoot a pilot for a Casserole Queens TV show. The setup was that we had to make a casserole for a Harlem church choir's potluck fundraiser. We immediately got excited thinking about all the eclectic flavors and different cuisines that Harlem had to offer, but the twist was that our church members had several dietary restrictions: no shellfish, no pork, no red meat. What a challenge! We decided on serving these remarkable eggplant rolls. Not only are they extremely delectable, they're also elegant and filling. Though the show didn't take off, we think we made out like bandits with this fabulous recipe! *Serves 8 to 10*

GLUTEN-FREE
VEGETARIAN!

2 (28-ounce) cans diced tomatoes

2 medium yellow onions, halved

½ cup (1 stick) unsalted butter

1½ teaspoons salt

2 eggplants, cut lengthwise into ⅛-inch slices

2 tablespoons olive oil

Cooking spray

1 cup quick-cooking grits

1½ cups vegetable stock (see page 194)

1 cup heavy cream

1½ teaspoons Creole Seasoning (page 189)

1 (5-ounce) package fresh baby spinach, chopped

1 cup shredded Parmesan cheese (4 ounces)

1 cup shredded mozzarella cheese (4 ounces)

1 In a heavy medium saucepan set over medium heat, combine the tomatoes, onion, and butter. Bring to a simmer and keep the sauce at a slow, steady simmer for about 45 minutes, or until it has thickened. Remove the pan from heat, discard the onion, and add 1 teaspoon of the salt.

2 Meanwhile, preheat the oven to 425°F.

3 Arrange the eggplant slices in a single layer on a nonstick baking sheet. Using a pastry brush, lightly brush both sides of each slice with the olive oil. Bake for 10 minutes, flip, and cook the second side for another 10 minutes.

4 Reduce the oven temperature to 350°F. Spray a 9 x 13-inch casserole dish with cooking spray.

5 In a medium saucepan set over medium-high heat, combine the grits, vegetable stock, heavy cream, the remaining ½ teaspoon of salt, and the Creole seasoning, and bring the mixture to a boil. Reduce the heat to low and simmer, stirring occasionally, for 5 minutes, or until thickened. Remove the pan from the heat and stir in the spinach, ½ cup of the Parmesan cheese, and ½ cup of the mozzarella cheese. Stir well.

6 Put 1 slice of eggplant on a work surface. Put 2 table-spoons of the grits mixture on the large end of the eggplant slice. Roll the eggplant from the large end toward the small end to enclose the grits. Put the eggplant roll seam side down in the prepared casserole dish. Repeat with the remaining eggplant slices and grits mixture. Pour the tomato sauce over the rolls and sprinkle the top with the remaining ½ cup of Parmesan cheese and the remaining ½ cup of mozzarella cheese.

7 Bake for 25 minutes or until heated through. Remove from the oven and let rest for 5 minutes before serving.

FREEZES WELL! For best results, prepare the casserole through step 6. Wrap in foil and freeze for up to 2 months. Thaw the casserole overnight in the refrigerator before baking as stated in the recipe. Note that casseroles that have not been completely thawed may take 15 to 30 minutes longer, so be sure to check for bubbling edges and a hot center.

RUSTIC
Polenta Casserole

This dish comes together fast for a simple weeknight meal, and it's also elegant enough to serve to any important guest. So the next time you get the unexpected call from your spouse saying that the boss is coming over for dinner, you will know what to serve! Pair it with our Panzanella Salad (page 134) for a delightful and filling vegetarian meal. *Serves 6*

GLUTEN-FREE

VEGETARIAN!

Cooking spray

1 teaspoon olive oil

2 cups chopped onion (about 2 onions)

3 cups (12 ounces) coarsely chopped shiitake mushrooms

2 garlic cloves, minced

1½ teaspoons salt

⅓ cup red wine

1 tablespoon tomato paste

1 tablespoon chopped fresh thyme

1 (15-ounce) can diced tomatoes

1 cup polenta

½ cup shredded Asiago cheese (2 ounces)

¼ teaspoon freshly ground black pepper

½ cup fresh goat cheese

1½ teaspoons unsalted butter, cut into small pieces

1 Preheat the oven to 400°F. Spray a 9 x 13-inch casserole dish with cooking spray.

2 Heat the oil in a medium sauté pan set over medium-high heat. Add the onions and cook for 8 minutes, until they start to brown. Add the mushrooms, garlic, and ½ teaspoon of the salt, and cook, stirring, for 4 minutes. Add the wine, tomato paste, and thyme and cook for 3 minutes. Stir in the tomatoes, reduce heat to medium, and cook for 10 minutes, or until thick.

3 Bring 4 cups of water to a boil in a medium saucepan. Stir in the polenta and the remaining 1 teaspoon of the salt. Reduce the heat to low and cook, stirring, for 20 to 30 minutes, or until thick.

4 Spread a third of the polenta into the prepared casserole dish. Spread half of the tomato sauce over the polenta and sprinkle with 2 tablespoons of the Asiago cheese and ⅛ teaspoon of the pepper. Crumble and

sprinkle half of the goat cheese across the casserole. Repeat the layers, ending with the last third of the polenta. Top with the remaining ¼ cup of the Asiago cheese and top with the butter.

5 Bake for 25 minutes, or until bubbly.

FREEZES WELL! For best results, prepare the casserole through step 4. Wrap in foil and freeze for up to 2 months. Thaw the casserole overnight in the refrigerator before baking as stated in the recipe. Note that casseroles that have not been completely thawed may take 15 to 30 minutes longer, so be sure to check for bubbling edges and a hot center.

ERIN'S SPECIAL GLUTEN-FREE
Corn Dog Casserole

Our dear friend Erin loves our corn dog casserole, which is in our first book. But she's discovered that her body can't handle gluten, and, sadly, the Jiffy mix we use contains

it. We didn't want her to have to do without delicious corn dog goodness, so this is a special version that we created for her! We swapped out the Jiffy for Bob's Red Mill Gluten Free Cornbread Mix, and we also decided to use uncured hotdogs, which are both nitrate- and preservative-free. It sure turned into a mighty fine dish! *Serves 8*

Cooking spray

2 tablespoons unsalted butter

2 celery ribs, minced

1 bunch green onions, green parts only, sliced

1½ pounds uncured hot dogs

1½ cups whole milk

2 large eggs

1 (20-ounce) bag Bob's Red Mill Gluten Free Cornbread Mix

2 teaspoons chopped fresh sage

¼ teaspoon salt

¼ teaspoon freshly ground black pepper

2 cups shredded sharp Cheddar cheese (8 ounces)

1 Preheat the oven to 400°F. Spray a 9 x 13-inch casserole dish with cooking spray.

2 In a large sauté pan set over medium-high heat, melt the butter. Add the celery and cook for 5 minutes. Add the onions and cook for 2 more minutes. Transfer the celery and onions to a large bowl and set aside.

3 Cut the hot dogs in half lengthwise, then cut into ½-inch-pieces. Sauté the dogs in the same pan, turning to brown on all sides, about 6 minutes. Transfer the hot dogs to the bowl with the celery and onions.

4 In a medium bowl, lightly beat together the milk and eggs. Add the cornbread mix, sage, salt, and pepper, and stir well. Add the hot dogs, celery, and onions and 1½ cups of the cheese and stir well. Pour the mixture into the prepared casserole dish. Sprinkle the remaining ½ cup of cheese over the top.

5 Bake for 30 minutes, or until the casserole is golden brown and has risen slightly. You want a nice golden-brown crust on top.

FREEZES WELL! **For best results, prepare the casserole through step 4. Wrap in foil and freeze for up to 2 months. Thaw the casserole overnight in the refrigerator before baking as stated in the recipe. Note that casseroles that have not been completely thawed may take 15 to 30 minutes longer, so be sure to check for bubbling edges and a hot center.**

This can easily be made VEGETARIAN by substituting your favorite vegetarian hot dog alternative for the regular hot dogs.

SPINACH AND GRUYÈRE
Soufflé

VEGETARIAN!

Canapés. En croûte. Flambé. Soufflé. Why do all those words with the little accent marks seem so intimidating? Technically, canapés are just tiny appetizers. *En croûte* ("in a crust") is basically just wrapping puff pastry around something. To flambé is to set fire to something. And the secret to a successful soufflé is to beat the heck out of some egg whites. Seriously, folks, if you've never made a soufflé before, don't be afraid. They are actually quite easy to make, and our recipe contains simple shortcuts to make the process easier on you. Traditionally, savory soufflés rely on a béchamel sauce (again another scary word with an accent mark), but we skip the sauce and just use eggs and cheese for the custard. What cheese you ask? Why Gruyère (with the accent mark) of course! *Serves 8*

2 tablespoons unsalted butter, plus more for the dish

2 tablespoons all-purpose flour, plus more for the dish

1 cup whole milk

¼ teaspoon cayenne pepper

¼ teaspoon ground nutmeg

½ teaspoon salt, plus a pinch more for the egg whites

½ teaspoon freshly ground black pepper

6 large egg yolks (see Note)

8 ounces fresh spinach

1½ cups Gruyère cheese (6 ounces)

6 large egg whites, at room temperature

1 **Preheat the oven to 375°F. Butter a 9 x 13-inch casserole dish and dust with flour.**

2 **In a medium saucepan set over medium heat, melt the butter. Add the flour and cook for 2 minutes, stirring constantly. Remove the pan from the heat and add the milk, cayenne, nutmeg, the ½ teaspoon of salt, and the pepper. Whisk well, making sure to get all the flour off the bottom of the pan. Return the pan to the heat and cook, whisking constantly, until the mixture is thick and smooth, 3 to 5 minutes. Remove the pan from the heat and add the egg yolks, spinach, and cheese. Stir well.**

3 **In a large bowl, whisk the egg whites with a pinch of salt until stiff peaks form.**

4 Whisk a quarter of the egg whites into the cheese mixture to lighten it, then gently fold in the rest of the egg whites. Pour the mixture into the prepared casserole dish. Bake for about 35 minutes, until the soufflé has risen and is firm to the touch. The key to *serving* a soufflé is to get it to the table before it falls. Have a serving tray right near the oven, or a trivet placed on the dinner table. That way, when the soufflé comes out, it can be served immediately with a large spoon.

This dish can be made GLUTEN-FREE by replacing the flour with a gluten-free all-purpose mix, either store bought (see page 15 for recommendations of our favorite brands) or homemade (see page 186 for our recipe).

Eggs separate more easily when cold, but the whites whip up better at room temperature.

THE GREAT PUMPKIN PASTA

There is something magical that happens in late September: pumpkin-flavored foods are suddenly everywhere you turn. There are pumpkin-spiced lattes, pumpkin breads, **VEGETARIAN!** pumpkin beer, and hold on . . . there are even pumpkin-flavored Pop-Tarts! To all of those things, we say, yes, please! And we continue to say yes until the end of November, when flavors turn to peppermint and gingerbread. We love the fall for this pumpkin explosion, and we decided that there's no need to wait until then to satisfy our craving. This amazing pasta delivers that pumpkin fix whenever we need it. *Serves 6*

Cooking spray

1 pound uncooked penne pasta

2 teaspoons olive oil

1 medium onion, finely chopped

2 garlic cloves, minced

2 small zucchini, halved lengthwise and sliced

1 bunch kale, thick stems removed and leaves coarsely chopped

1 teaspoon dried sage

½ teaspoon dried thyme

2 teaspoons salt

½ teaspoon ground cinnamon

1 (15-ounce) can pumpkin puree (not pumpkin pie filling)

1 cup part-skim ricotta cheese

½ cup vegetable stock (see page 194)

1 cup shredded Parmesan cheese (4 ounces)

¼ cup pumpkin seeds, toasted

1 Preheat the oven to 400°F. Spray a 9 x 13-inch casserole dish with cooking spray.

2 In a large pot, cook the pasta according to the package directions. Drain and set aside.

3 In a large sauté pan set over medium-high heat, heat the olive oil. Add the onion and garlic and cook for about 5 minutes, until softened. Add the zucchini, kale, sage, thyme, salt, and cinnamon and sauté for about 5 minutes, or until the kale wilts. Stir in the pumpkin and ricotta cheese. Add the pasta and the vegetable stock to the pan and mix well. Spoon the mixture into the prepared casserole dish and sprinkle the top with the Parmesan cheese and pumpkin seeds.

4 Bake for 10 to 15 minutes, until heated through.

This dish can be made GLUTEN-FREE by using a gluten-free brand of pasta, such as Gilda's Gluten Free House La Rosa Penne. See page 15 for recommendations of our other favorite brands.

The Nelly
FRITTATA

Get it? Nelly Frittata . . . Nelly Furtado . . . funny, right? All kidding aside, this is one serious frittata. Packed with asparagus, thyme, onions, and Parmesan cheese, this frittata is bursting with flavor and is naturally gluten-free, vegetarian, and diabetic-friendly! Fabulous, healthy, and all around awesome, just like Nelly herself! Serve with your favorite salad greens and our Lemon Parmesan Dressing (page 117) or our A Few of Sandy's Favorite Things Orzo Pasta Salad (page 136) for a light dinner or special brunch. *Serves 6 to 8*

GLUTEN-FREE

DIABETIC-FRIENDLY

VEGETARIAN!

1 tablespoon unsalted butter

1 tablespoon vegetable oil

1 bunch asparagus, trimmed and chopped

1 medium onion, cut in half and sliced

1/2 cup grated Parmesan cheese (2 ounces)

8 large eggs

1/4 cup whole milk

1 teaspoon salt

1/2 teaspoon freshly ground black pepper

1 tablespoon chopped fresh thyme

1 Preheat the oven to 350°F.

2 In a 12-inch ovenproof skillet set over medium-high heat, heat the butter and oil. Add the asparagus and onion and sauté for 12 to 14 minutes, or until the onion is tender. Remove the pan from the heat, and stir in 2 tablespoons of the cheese.

3 In a medium bowl, whisk together the eggs, milk, salt, and pepper until well blended. Pour over the vegetable mixture.

4 Bake for 13 to 15 minutes, or until set. Increase the oven temperature to Broil, and broil for 1 to 2 minutes, or until the edges are lightly browned. Remove the pan from the oven and sprinkle with the remaining 2 tablespoons of cheese and the thyme. Serve hot.

BUTTERNUT SQUASH GRATIN
with Asiago Cheese and Toasted Pine Nuts

When Sandy and Crystal really like something they see on a menu, they can't help but exclaim, "I want to eat that with my face!" Silly? Yes. But it gets the point across, don't you think? The nuttiness of the Asiago cheese and the savory flavor of the sage balance out the sweetness of the squash—making one harmonious dish! Serve along with a simple green salad with our Balsamic Vinaigrette (page 122) and a side of our Braised Endive Gratin (page 147). Delish! *Serves 8 to 10*

GLUTEN-FREE

DIABETIC-FRIENDLY

VEGETARIAN!

¼ cup (½ stick) unsalted butter

2 medium butternut squash, peeled, seeded, and cut into ¾-inch cubes

2 tablespoons olive oil

1 teaspoon salt, plus more to taste

½ teaspoon freshly ground black pepper, plus more to taste

2 leeks, white and pale green parts, cleaned and thinly sliced (3 cups)

1½ teaspoons chopped fresh sage

1½ cups Asiago cheese, shredded (8 ounces)

1 cup heavy cream

½ cup pine nuts, toasted

1 Preheat the oven to 375°F. Grease a 9 x 13-inch casserole dish with 1 tablespoon of the butter.

2 Put the butternut squash and olive oil in a large bowl, sprinkle with the 1 teaspoon of salt and the ½ teaspoon of pepper, and toss to coat. Spread the squash out on a large rimmed baking sheet. Roast, stirring occasionally, for 35 minutes, or until just tender and beginning to brown. Remove the pan from the oven and set aside to cool slightly.

3 In a medium saucepan set over medium-low heat, melt the remaining 3 tablespoons butter, then add the leeks, sage, and salt and pepper to taste. Cook, stirring, until tender, about 10 minutes.

4 Spread half of the leek mixture in the bottom of the prepared casserole dish. Cover with half of the squash and half of the cheese. Repeat the layers of leeks, squash, and cheese.

5 Pour the cream evenly over the casserole and bake for 25 minutes. Pull the casserole out of the oven and sprinkle the top with pine nuts. Return the pan to the oven and bake for 15 more minutes, or until bubbling around the edges.

SHEPHERDLESS PIE

GLUTEN-FREE

VEGETARIAN!

We're never sheepish about serving our meatless version of this traditional comfort food, and you shouldn't be either. The kidney beans satisfy meat lovers with their hearty flavor, while sweet potatoes and winter vegetables provide a nice twist on a classic dish. Your flock won't want to stray far from the dinner table when this is on the menu! Serve along with our Dill Bread (page 160) to complete the meal. *Serves 6*

Cooking spray

2 teaspoons olive oil

1 onion, chopped

2 celery ribs, diced

1 garlic clove, minced

1 small butternut squash, peeled, seeded, and cut into 3/4-inch cubes

3 carrots, chopped

1 cup broccoli, chopped

1 (15.5-ounce) can kidney beans

2 red bell peppers, seeded and chopped

1 (15-ounce) can diced tomatoes

1 teaspoon chopped fresh parsley

2 tablespoons cornstarch

4 sweet potatoes

1 cup vegetable stock, homemade (see page 194) or store bought, warmed

1 Preheat the oven to 400°F. Spray a 9 x 13-inch casserole dish with cooking spray.

2 In a large sauté pan set over medium heat, heat the olive oil. Add the onion, celery, and garlic, and cook for 5 minutes. Add the squash, carrots, and broccoli. Cook for 10 minutes, or until the carrots start to soften. Add the beans, peppers, and tomatoes. Bring the mixture to a simmer and cook until the squash is just tender, 15 minutes. Stir in the parsley and cornstarch. Transfer to the prepared casserole dish.

3 Meanwhile, pierce each sweet potato several times with a fork. Bake them for 45 minutes, or until tender. Let cool until they can be handled. Peel the sweet potatoes and put them in a large bowl. Add the warm vegetable stock and whisk until smooth. Spread the mashed sweet potatoes over the stew.

4 Bake for 15 minutes, or until the top is a lovely golden brown.

FARRO, WILD MUSHROOM,
and Walnut Casserole

Farro—which is sometimes called spelt or emmer wheat—is one of the first grains ever

DIABETIC-FRIENDLY

VEGETARIAN!

discovered. It is a unique alternative to pasta and rice because of its distinctive chewy texture and is healthy, tasty, and versatile. Higher in fiber and protein than wheat, farro is also especially rich in magnesium and B vitamins. Its nutty flavor makes it a welcome addition to soups and salads, and it serves as the star of this savory stuffing-type dish. *Serves 8*

Cooking spray

1½ cups uncooked farro

1 teaspoon salt

2 tablespoons olive oil

2 medium onions, chopped

6 cups sliced fresh shiitake
mushroom caps (about
12 ounces)

1 tablespoon chopped
fresh thyme

1 tablespoon chopped
fresh sage

½ teaspoon freshly ground
black pepper

½ cup white wine

⅔ cup dried cranberries

⅔ cup walnuts, chopped

1 Preheat the oven to 350°F. Spray a 9 x 13-inch casserole dish with cooking spray.

2 In a large pot set over high heat, combine 5 cups of water with the farro and ½ teaspoon salt. Bring the mixture to a boil. Reduce the heat to medium and simmer for 15 minutes, or until the farro is al dente. Drain and set aside.

3 In a large saucepan set over medium heat, heat 1 tablespoon of the oil. Add the onions and cook, stirring, for 2 minutes. Reduce the heat to medium-low and cook until the onions are tender and lightly browned, 15 to 20 minutes.

4 In a large skillet set over medium-high heat, heat the remaining 1 tablespoon oil. Add the mushrooms, thyme, sage, pepper, and the remaining ½ teaspoon salt. Cook, stirring occasionally, for 5 minutes, until the mushrooms have released their juices. Add the wine and cook for 4 to 5 minutes, or until the liquid evaporates. Add the mushroom mixture, onions, and the cranberries to the cooked farro and stir well.

5 Put the mixture into the prepared casserole dish, sprinkle the walnuts over the top, and cover the dish with foil. Bake for 30 minutes, until all the liquid has been absorbed and the farro is tender. Let stand for 5 minutes before serving.

FREEZES WELL! For best results, prepare the casserole through step 4. Wrap in foil and freeze for up to 2 months. Thaw the casserole overnight in the refrigerator before baking as stated in the recipe. Note that casseroles that have not been completely thawed may take 15 to 30 minutes longer, so be sure to check for bubbling edges and a hot center.

This dish can be made GLUTEN-FREE by substituting a gluten-free wild rice blend, such as Lundberg's, for the farro.

GREEN CHILI
and Chicken Bake

This Tex-Mex favorite combines the full flavor of Manchego and the creamy, mild flavor of Monterey Jack to create a sophisticated twist on a traditional chicken-and-rice dish. We also go the extra mile by toasting the rice, both to impart a nutty flavor and to reduce the total cooking time. Dotting the rice with butter adds flavor and helps provide a nice golden color when broiling. *Serves 6*

Cooking spray

2 tablespoons olive oil

3 boneless, skinless whole chicken breasts, cut into cubes

1 teaspoon salt, plus more for the chicken

½ teaspoon freshly ground black pepper, plus more for the chicken

3 (4-ounce) cans diced green chilies

1 (14.5-ounce) can stewed tomatoes (Mexican-style, if available)

1 (8-ounce) can tomato sauce

1½ teaspoons chopped fresh oregano

1½ cups chopped onion (about 2 small onions)

2 garlic cloves, minced

1 jalapeño pepper, seeds removed, and chopped

1 teaspoon ground cumin

1 tablespoon chili powder

1½ cups long-grain rice

3 cups chicken stock, homemade (see page 192) or store bought

1 Preheat the oven to 375°F. Spray a 9 x 13-inch casserole dish with cooking spray.

2 In a large sauté pan set over medium-high heat, heat 1 tablespoon of the olive oil. Season the chicken with salt and pepper and put it in the pan. Cook, stirring, until it's no longer pink, about 8 minutes. Add the green chilies, stewed tomatoes, and tomato sauce. Season with the 1 teaspoon of salt, the ½ teaspoon of black pepper, and the oregano. Pour the mixture into the prepared casserole dish.

3 Bake the casserole for 20 minutes. Remove the dish from the oven and set the oven to Broil.

4 Meanwhile, in the same pot set over medium-high heat, heat the remaining 1 tablespoon of olive oil. Add the onions, garlic, jalapeño, cumin, and chili powder. Sauté until the onions are golden, 5 minutes. Stir in the rice and continue to cook until it is lightly toasted, about 5 minutes. Add enough chicken stock to cover the mixture, scraping up the brown bits on the bottom of the pan. Cover pan with a lid and cook until the rice is done, about 45 minutes.

¼ cup (½ stick) butter, cut into small pieces

1 cup shredded Monterey Jack cheese (4 ounces)

1 cup shredded Manchego cheese (4 ounces)

2 tablespoons chopped fresh cilantro

½ cup crushed corn tortilla chips

5 Spread the cooked rice over the baked chicken in the casserole dish and dot with butter. Broil until the top of the rice is golden and crispy, about 6 minutes. Remove the dish from the oven and sprinkle the top with the Monterey Jack and Manchego cheeses. Return the dish to the oven and broil again until the cheese is melted, about 2 minutes.

6 Sprinkle with the cilantro and the crushed chips and serve.

FREEZES WELL! For best results, prepare the casserole through step 2. Cover with foil and freeze for up to 2 months. Thaw the casserole overnight in the refrigerator. The next day, prepare the rice topping (step 4) and broil as stated in the recipe. Note that casseroles that have not been completely thawed may take 15 to 30 minutes longer, so be sure to check for bubbling edges and a hot center.

NAME THAT
CASSEROLE!

In Seven
Ingredients or Less

The clock is ticking. Dinner is approaching. Stomachs are growling. No sweat! These tried-and-true casseroles combine just seven ingredients or less—not counting salt, pepper, or oil—for speedy meals that you'll feel great about serving. With our make-ahead tips and cooking shortcuts, these classic favorites can be on your table in no time. Who would have thought that leftover mashed potatoes could make a crust for pizza? Or that frozen tater tots would be the crowning glory of a meaty casserole? We Queens are always coming up with crafty and tasty ways to get dinner on the table!

- **SUPER-SIMPLE SPINACH-STUFFED SHELLS**
- **MONTEREY CHICKEN AND RICE**
- **MEXICAN SPAGHETTI**
- **MASHED POTATO PIZZA**
- **CHICKEN CASSEROLE: A COOK FAMILY FAVORITE**

- **SAVORY FRENCH ONION TART**
- **TUNA TOMATO BAKE**
- **TATER TOT CASSEROLE**
- **RAVIOLI LASAGNA**
- **CARIBBEAN SHRIMP CASSEROLE**

SUPER-SIMPLE
Spinach-Stuffed Shells

We Queens are always on the lookout for easy go-to meal solutions. Our latest obsession  happens to be these super-simple spinach-stuffed shells. They're meatless, easy, kid-friendly, and delicious! When you remove the foil for the last 10 minutes of baking, you can quickly throw together our Broccoli Rabe with Shallots (page 142) for a tasty sidekick. You're welcome! *Serves 8*

Cooking spray

3 cups shredded Italian cheese mixture (12 ounces)

2 (10-ounce) boxes chopped spinach, thawed and well drained

1 (15-ounce) container ricotta cheese

4 ounces cream cheese, softened

2 large eggs, beaten

1/2 teaspoon salt

1/2 teaspoon freshly ground black pepper

1 (24-ounce) jar marinara sauce, or 3 cups homemade (page 197; see Note)

1 (12-ounce) box jumbo pasta shells

1 Preheat the oven to 350°F. Spray a 9 x 13-inch casserole dish with cooking spray .

2 In a large bowl, combine 2 cups of the Italian cheese with the spinach, ricotta cheese, cream cheese, eggs, salt, and pepper.

3 Pour about 1 1/2 cups of the marinara sauce into the prepared casserole dish, spreading the sauce around to cover the bottom of the dish.

4 In a large pot of boiling salted water, cook the pasta shells for 8 minutes, or until al dente. Rinse the shells under cool water to stop the cooking process. Stuff the shells immediately so they won't start sticking together. Stuff each shell with 1/2 cup of the cheese-and-spinach mixture. Put the filled shells into the casserole dish. Cover the pasta with the remaining 1 1/2 cups of sauce. Sprinkle the remaining 1 cup of Italian cheese on top.

5 Cover the dish with foil and bake for 50 minutes. Remove the foil and bake for 10 minutes more. Remove the casserole from the oven and let it stand for 5 minutes before serving.

FREEZES WELL! For best results, prepare the casserole through step 4. Cover with foil and freeze for up to 2 months. Thaw the casserole overnight in the refrigerator before baking as stated in the recipe. Note that casseroles that have not been completely thawed may take 15 to 30 minutes longer, so be sure to check for bubbling edges and a hot center.

This recipe can be made GLUTEN-FREE by using a gluten-free pasta. See page 15 for recommendations of our favorite brands.

On a weekend when you have some time and find yourself prepping items for the week, do yourself a solid and make our homemade Marinara Sauce (page 197). Freeze several containers and thaw as needed. Store-bought sauces work fine in a pinch, but your flavors will be truly elevated by using your own sauce. Besides, the time you'll save making this superquick dish will allow you the luxury of making sauces for storage.

MONTEREY CHICKEN AND RICE

This casserole comes together in a snap, so do yourself a favor and go ahead and double up the recipe. Casseroles prepared ahead of time and stored in the freezer are an easy solution for providing a home-cooked meal on a busy day. And this dish is so flavorful, your family will be happy to see it in frequent rotation. One thing to note is that this recipe calls for a crispy corn chip topping. Wait to add it until right before baking, instead of putting it on before freezing. Corn chips tend to get soggy when frozen, and you'll miss out on the delightful crunch. *Serves 6*

Cooking spray

1 (8-ounce) package cream cheese, softened

1 (3-pound) roasted chicken, boned and shredded (see page 200)

3 cups cooked rice (see page 199)

1 cup shredded Monterey Jack cheese (4 ounces)

1 (4-ounce) can diced green chilies

1 (10¾-ounce) can cream of chicken soup, or 1½ cups homemade (see page 196)

1 teaspoon salt

½ teaspoon freshly ground black pepper

¾ cup corn chips, coarsely crushed

1 Preheat the oven to 350°F. Spray a 9 x 13-inch casserole dish with cooking spray.

2 In a large bowl, stir the cream cheese until smooth. Add the chicken, rice, cheese, chilies, soup, salt, and pepper. Mix well and pour into the prepared casserole dish.

3 Sprinkle the top of the casserole with the corn chips. Bake for 25 to 30 minutes, until golden brown and bubbling around the edges.

FREEZES WELL! For best results, prepare the casserole through step 2. Wrap in foil and freeze for up to 2 months. Thaw the casserole overnight in the refrigerator. The next day, sprinkle the top of the casserole with the corn chips and bake as stated in the recipe. Note that casseroles that have not been completely thawed may take 15 to 30 minutes longer, so be sure to check for bubbling edges and a hot center.

This dish is GLUTEN-FREE as long as the cream of chicken soup is gluten-free. See page 196 for our recipe or page 15 for recommendations of our favorite brands.

MEXICAN
Spaghetti

Another name for this great dish is fideo, which is also the Spanish word for vermicelli. Ask anyone from Sandy's neck of the woods in the Rio Grande Valley about it, and you'll likely get a chuckle and their family's favorite recipe. There is a version called *sopa de fideo*, which is typically a chicken soup prepared with some mixture of fideo, tomatoes, cilantro, jalapeños, and cumin. Our recipe uses fideo as a flavorful bed for any type of prepared chicken, beef, or pork dish. But don't fret if you don't eat meat. The fideo itself is filling enough for a main course. You will just need to replace the chicken broth with a vegetable broth to make it truly vegetarian. If you are unable to find fideo, you can use vermicelli or fine egg noodles. *Serves 8*

Cooking spray

1 teaspoon olive oil

1 small onion, finely chopped

1/2 red bell pepper, chopped

1 (8-ounce) box fideo

3/4 cup chicken stock, homemade (see page 192) or store bought

3/4 cup tomato sauce

2 garlic cloves, minced

1/2 teaspoon ground cumin

1 teaspoon salt

1 Preheat the oven to 350°F. Spray a 9 x 13-inch casserole dish with cooking spray.

2 In a large saucepan set over medium heat, heat the olive oil. Add the onion and bell pepper and cook, stirring, until translucent, about 4 minutes. Add the fideo and cook until lightly toasted, about 5 minutes. Add the chicken stock, tomato sauce, garlic, cumin, and salt. Pour the mixture into the prepared casserole dish.

3 Bake for 30 minutes, or until most of the liquid has been cooked out.

This recipe can be made GLUTEN-FREE by using a gluten-free pasta. See page 15 for recommendations of our favorite brands.

This dish can be made VEGETARIAN by substituting vegetable broth for the chicken broth.

MASHED POTATO
Pizza

Turn your leftover mashed potatoes into a delicious crust for a tasty casserole spin on a deep-dish pizza! Don't worry if your mashed potatoes were seasoned with herbs or Parmesan cheese—we think seasoning will only enhance the flavor of the "crust." You can always make a fresh batch of spuds for this recipe, so check out our recipe opposite. *Serves 8 to 10*

GLUTEN-FREE

1 tablespoon olive oil

3 cups mashed potatoes, leftover or homemade (recipe follows)

2½ cups fresh or frozen broccoli florets (thawed and drained if frozen)

2 Roma tomatoes, chopped

2 cups shredded sharp Cheddar cheese (8 ounces)

6 slices bacon, cooked and crumbled

3 green onions, green parts only, sliced, for garnish

1 Preheat the oven to 350°F.

2 Brush a 9 x 13-inch casserole dish with ½ tablespoon of the olive oil and press the mashed potatoes along the bottom. Brush the top of the potatoes with the remaining ½ tablespoon olive oil. Bake for 30 minutes, or until lightly browned. Remove the crust from the oven, and keep the oven on.

3 Cover the potato crust evenly with the broccoli, tomatoes, cheese, and bacon. Bake the pizza for 15 to 20 more minutes, or until the cheese has melted. Garnish with the green onions, slice up, and serve.

Mashed Potatoes

MAKES 4 CUPS

2 pounds russet potatoes, peeled and cut into chunks
Salt
3 tablespoons unsalted butter
¾ cup heavy cream, warmed
Freshly ground black pepper

1 Put the potatoes in a saucepan and cover them with cold, salted water.

2 Set the pan over high heat and bring to a boil.

3 Reduce the heat to low and simmer until the potatoes are tender, about 30 minutes.

4 Drain the potatoes and mash them with the butter and cream until smooth.

5 Season with salt and pepper to taste.

It's easy to add depth to a multitude of dishes by simply roasting garlic cloves. For example, you can mash them up in your potatoes, spread them onto your pizza, blend them into a compound butter, toss them with pasta, or just spread them over French bread. They're very mild and quite sweet! Here's how you do it:

Preheat the oven to 400°F. Cut the top ¼ inch off a head of garlic so that the tops of each individual clove are exposed. Put the head of garlic on a large piece of heavy aluminum foil. Drizzle the top of the garlic with about 2 teaspoons of extra-virgin olive oil. Tightly wrap the garlic in the foil and roast for about 30 minutes. The garlic should be soft, fragrant, and golden. It will keep in the refrigerator for up to 5 days.

CHICKEN CASSEROLE:
A Cook Family Favorite

Many recipes are culinary heirlooms, passed down from generation to generation. This Cook family recipe is just such a thing. As far back as Crystal can trace, the source of this casserole is her great-aunt Eulene, and it was a dish beloved by both her aunt Mary Ann and her uncle Tommy. Today, Tommy and Mary Ann's children are preparing it for their kids, making it one of their favorites! We hope this can now become a favorite with your family, too! This casserole goes especially well with our Dill Bread (page 160). *Serves 8*

Cooking spray

2 (10¾-ounce) cans chicken stock, or homemade (page 192)

4 boneless, skinless whole chicken breasts

½ cup (1 stick) unsalted butter

2 medium onions, chopped

1 (8-ounce) package herb-seasoned stuffing mix

1 tablespoon dried sage

1 teaspoon salt

½ teaspoon freshly ground black pepper

2 (10.5-ounce) cans cream of chicken soup, or 2½ cups homemade (see page 196)

1 Preheat the oven to 400°F. Spray a 9 x 13-inch casserole dish with cooking spray.

2 In a large saucepan set over low heat, bring the chicken stock to a simmer. Add the chicken breasts, cover with a lid, and poach them for 15 to 20 minutes, or until they are tender and the meat no longer shows sign of pink when sliced at the thickest part. Remove the pan from the heat and let the chicken cool in the poaching liquid. Reserve 2 cups of the cooking liquid. Cut the chicken into small cubes.

3 In a large skillet set over medium-high heat, melt the butter. Add the onions and cook, stirring, until translucent, about 5 minutes. Add 1 cup of the reserved poaching liquid, the stuffing mix, sage, salt, and pepper.

4 In another medium saucepan set over medium-low heat, combine the cream of chicken soup and the remaining 1 cup of poaching liquid. Heat for about 5 minutes.

5 Put the chicken in the bottom of the prepared casserole dish. Pour the soup mixture over the chicken and top with the stuffing mixture.

6 Bake for 30 minutes, or until the casserole is heated through and the edges are bubbling.

FREEZES WELL! **For best results, prepare the casserole through step 5. Cover with foil and freeze for up to 2 months. Thaw the casserole overnight in the refrigerator before baking as stated in the recipe. Note that casseroles that have not been completely thawed may take 15 to 30 minutes longer, so be sure to check for bubbling edges and a hot center.**

This recipe can be made GLUTEN-FREE by using a gluten-free stuffing mix and a gluten-free cream of chicken soup. See page 15 for recommendations of our favorite brands.

SAVORY FRENCH ONION TART

During Sandy's days in culinary school, she learned how just a few simple ingredients can transform themselves into an elegant masterpiece. This simple onion tart is a perfect example. It has a thin, flaky crust, a creamy caramelized onion filling, and a delicious topping of Gruyère cheese. With a "touch" of crumbled bacon, this meal is over the top! And even though tarts are great cut up into small pieces for use at parties, we prefer serving ourselves a larger slice along with a simple green salad dressed in our homemade Balsamic Vinaigrette dressing (page 122). Tuesday night just became date night! *Serves 8*

2 tablespoons unsalted butter

4 onions, chopped

1 pound bacon, cooked and crumbled

5 large eggs

3½ cups whole milk

1 tablespoon fresh thyme, chopped

1 teaspoon salt

½ teaspoon freshly ground black pepper

2 pie crusts, homemade (page 187) or store bought

1 cup grated Gruyère cheese (4 ounces)

1 Preheat the oven to 400°F.

2 In a large sauté pan set over medium heat, melt butter, then add the onions and cook for 5 minutes, or until softened, but do not let them brown. Add the bacon and cook for about 5 minutes.

3 In a small bowl, whisk together the eggs, milk, thyme, salt, and pepper.

4 Line a 9 x 13-inch casserole dish with the pie crust and prick the bottom with a fork. Spread the onions and bacon in the casserole dish and sprinkle with the cheese. Pour the egg mixture over the top.

5 Bake for 25 to 30 minutes, or until the top is golden.

This dish can be made GLUTEN-FREE by replacing the pie crust with a gluten-free pie crust, either store bought or homemade (see page 187 for our recipe).

TUNA TOMATO
Bake

We don't care what people say . . . we love a good tuna noodle casserole! In our last book, we took the more traditional route, but with this dish, we went a little avant-garde! From the smokiness and color provided by the paprika, to the fresh flavors of the ripe tomatoes, this casserole leaves diners wowed and wondering what is next. How about dessert? We think that our Frozen Lemon Dessert (page 178) would be just the ticket! *Serves 6*

Cooking spray

2 (5-ounce) cans tuna, packed in water and drained

1½ cups mayonnaise

1 small onion, finely chopped

2 teaspoons smoked paprika

½ teaspoon salt

½ teaspoon freshly ground black pepper

1 (12-ounce) package wide egg noodles

8 to 10 plum tomatoes, sliced ¼ inch thick

1 cup shredded Cheddar cheese (4 ounces)

1 Preheat the oven to 375°F. Spray a 9 x 13-inch casserole dish with cooking spray.

2 In a medium bowl, combine the tuna, mayonnaise, onion, paprika, salt, and pepper.

3 In a large pot, cook the noodles according to the package directions. Drain and return the noodles to the saucepan. Add the tuna mixture to the noodles and stir well.

4 Put half of the noodle mixture in the prepared casserole dish and top with half of the tomatoes and half of the cheese. Press down slightly. Repeat the layers.

5 Bake for 20 minutes, or until the cheese is melted and the casserole is heated through.

This recipe can be made GLUTEN-FREE by using gluten-free noodles. See page 15 for recommendations of our favorite brands.

TATER TOT
Casserole

Um, what's not to love about this dish? Did you read the name? Tater tots and a casserole—that's the best thing we've ever heard of! Ground beef and a creamy mushroom mixture are topped off with Cheddar cheese and tater tots. Yep, you keep the tots for the top so that they can crisp up and make a crunchy layer above the cheesy center. We kept this dish simple, but it is one of those dishes that can be easily modified to include whatever else you may have on hand. For example, add onions and garlic when browning the beef for an extra layer of flavor, or spice it up with some taco seasoning and chopped bell peppers. Not a mushroom fan? No problem! Substitute some chopped celery and cream of celery soup. It's that easy! Anyone who has ever cooked a casserole has to have some improvising skills. You know, like nunchuku skills, bow hunting skills, computer hacking skills. (Come on, you really didn't think we could stop ourselves from making a *Napoleon Dynamite* reference in a tater tot casserole recipe, did ya?) *Serves* 10

Cooking spray

2 pounds lean ground beef

1½ teaspoons salt

1 teaspoon freshly ground black pepper

¼ cup (½ stick) unsalted butter

1 pound button mushrooms, sliced

1 (10.5-ounce) can cream of mushroom soup, or 1½ cups homemade (page 195)

2 cups shredded Cheddar cheese (8 ounces)

1 (2-pound) package frozen tater tots

1 Preheat the oven to 350°F. Spray a 9 x 13-inch casserole dish with cooking spray.

2 In a large sauté pan set over medium-high heat, combine the ground beef, 1 teaspoon of the salt, and ½ teaspoon of the pepper. Cook, breaking up any lumps with the back of a spoon, until the beef is browned through, about 8 minutes. Drain off the grease and place the beef in the prepared casserole dish.

3 Wipe out the sauté pan and return it to the heat. Melt the butter, then add the mushrooms. Cook, stirring, until the mushrooms release their juices and start to brown, about 6 minutes. Season with the remaining ½ teaspoon of salt and the remaining ½ teaspoon of pepper. Spread

the mushrooms over the beef, and then spread cream of mushroom soup on top of the mushrooms. Sprinkle the cheese over the casserole and top with the tater tots.

4 Cover the dish with foil and bake for 45 minutes. Uncover the dish and bake for 15 minutes more, or until golden brown on top.

FREEZES WELL! For best results, prepare the casserole through step 3. Wrap in foil and freeze for up to 2 months. Thaw the casserole overnight in the refrigerator before baking as stated in the recipe. Note that casseroles that have not been completely thawed may take 15 to 30 minutes longer, so be sure to check for bubbling edges and a hot center.

RAVIOLI LASAGNA

If it looks like a duck, quacks like a duck, then it must be a duck—right? Same idea applies here . . . if it looks like lasagna, tastes like lasagna, then it must be lasagna! This ingenious casserole looks and tastes just like the real thing, but it requires only a fraction of the prep time. By using convenience items, you can make an impressive dish for your family and friends with little time and effort. *Serves 8*

VEGETARIAN!

Cooking spray

1 (24-ounce) jar marinara sauce, or 3 cups homemade (see page 197)

1 pound fresh spinach, chopped

2 tablespoons dried parsley

2 teaspoons salt

1 teaspoon freshly ground black pepper

1 (15-ounce) container ricotta cheese

1 (8-ounce) container cottage cheese

1 (25-ounce) package frozen cheese-filled ravioli

3 cups shredded Italian cheese mix (12 ounces)

1 Preheat the oven to 350°F. Spray a 9 x 13-inch casserole dish with cooking spray.

2 In a large saucepan set over medium heat, heat the marinara sauce until heated through, about 10 minutes. Add the spinach, 1 tablespoon parsley, salt, and pepper, and cook for about 3 minutes, or until the spinach has wilted. Set aside.

3 In a medium-size bowl, combine the ricotta cheese, cottage cheese, and remaining 1 tablespoon parsley. Set aside.

4 Pour a third of the marinara mixture into the bottom of the prepared dish. Arrange half of the frozen ravioli in a single layer on top. Spread half of the ricotta mixture over the ravioli and sprinkle with 1 cup of the shredded cheese. Repeat the layers, ending with the remaining marinara mixture. Sprinkle the remaining 1 cup shredded cheese over the top.

5 Bake for 30 minutes, or until cheese starts to brown and the sauce is bubbling around the edges. If the cheese starts to get too brown, cover the dish with foil.

FREEZES WELL! For best results, prepare the casserole through step 4. Wrap in foil and freeze for up to 2 months. Thaw the casserole overnight in the refrigerator before baking as stated in the recipe. Note that casseroles that have not been completely thawed may take 15 to 30 minutes longer, so be sure to check for bubbling edges and a hot center.

CARIBBEAN SHRIMP
Casserole

The Queens simply adore shrimp, and for two main reasons: they are very versatile and relatively easy to cook, and they absorb flavors quickly, so dinners can come together  in a flash! From prep to table, this dish takes less than 40 minutes, while your family will think you've been slaving away in the kitchen all day. (So maybe use the extra time you're NOT cooking to get a manicure!) For a balanced meal, pair with our Corn Pudding (page 144). *Serves 6*

Cooking spray

2 tablespoons unsalted butter

1 large green bell pepper, chopped

2½ pounds fresh or frozen shrimp, peeled and deveined (thawed if frozen)

1 (28-ounce) can crushed tomatoes

2 teaspoons chili powder

½ teaspoon dried thyme

1 teaspoon salt

1½ teaspoons freshly ground black pepper

2 cups cooked rice (see page 199)

1 Preheat the oven to 350°F. Spray a 9 x 13-inch casserole dish with cooking spray.

2 In a large skillet set over medium-high heat, melt the butter. Add the green bell pepper and cook, stirring, until soft, about 5 minutes. Reduce the heat to medium and add the shrimp. Cook for 3 minutes, or until the shrimp turns pink. Stir in the crushed tomatoes, chili powder, thyme, salt, and pepper. Increase the heat to high and bring to a boil, then reduce the heat to medium and cook for 10 minutes.

3 Spread the rice in the bottom of the prepared casserole dish and press down firmly. Pour the shrimp mixture over the rice.

4 Bake for 15 minutes, or until heated through.

Casseroles can be chock-full of yummy, nutritious veggies, but sometimes there's just no substitute for fresh, leafy greens. And salads can be just as delicious and tempting as a heaping dish of our signature potpie. Or at least a really close second. To get the most out of this chapter, make sure to look for our pairing tips. Our Tomato and Feta Salad (page 125) goes great with our Moussaka (page 54). Try the Panzanella Salad (page 134) with an Italian casserole. The combinations of flavorful goodness seem endless!

* **DRESS IT UP!**
  Lemon Parmesan Dressing
  Creamy Chipotle Ranch Dressing
  Fiesta French Dressing
  Thousand Island Dressing
  Balsamic Vinaigrette
  Greek Dressing

* **CRYSTAL'S WEDGE SALAD WITH BACON AND BLUE CHEESE DRESSING**

* **TOMATO AND FETA SALAD**

* **PINT-SIZE CAPRESE SALAD**

* **TOMATO AND AVOCADO SALAD**

* **JAYNE'S MARINATED VEGETABLE SALAD**

* **HARGILL'S BUNCO CLUB 7-LAYER SALAD**

* **CRYSTAL'S MAY-I-HAVE-MORE-MAYO POTATO SALAD**

* **COMMUNITY-BUILDING WARM BACON SPINACH SALAD**

* **JAYNE'S SEAFOOD PASTA SALAD**

* **BROCCOLI SALAD**

* **PANZANELLA SALAD**

* **CORNBREAD SALAD TWO WAYS**

* **A FEW OF SANDY'S FAVORITE THINGS ORZO PASTA SALAD**

* **TOMATO, GOAT CHEESE, AND QUINOA SALAD**

Dress It Up!

Some casseroles are more complex than others, but overall, the main goal of a casserole is to make weeknight dinners or entertaining easier on you. That way, you have more time to enjoy dinner with your friends and family. Most casseroles are a meal on their own, so pairing them with a simple salad and some bread is always an easy solution! The Queens suggest that you keep a bag of your favorite mixed greens on hand and take flavor cues from your casserole to match your dressings! Having something Italian? Serve it with a Lemon Parmesan Dressing (opposite). Having Mexican? Go for a Creamy Chipotle Ranch Dressing (page 118). It's that easy! Whether you like vinaigrette or the creamy stuff, you only need a few simple ingredients on hand (and a couple of minutes) to make some yourself. Here are a few of our favorites.

LEMON PARMESAN
Dressing

This simple dressing is great paired with most Italian fare or with delicate dishes, such as seafood. The fresh flavor of lemon and the heartiness of the Parmesan is what makes this dressing sing. If possible, use a very finely grated Parmigiano Reggiano, as it will dissolve better. We also love this dressing when brushed on grilled vegetables, tossed in pasta salad, or drizzled over roasted new potatoes. *Makes 1 cup*

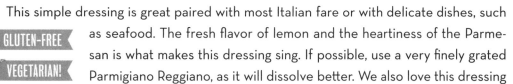

GLUTEN-FREE

VEGETARIAN!

¾ cup vegetable oil

¼ cup fresh lemon juice

2 tablespoons grated Parmigiano Reggiano cheese

1 garlic clove, minced

¼ teaspoon sugar

¾ teaspoon salt

1 In a jar with a tight-fitting lid, combine the oil, lemon juice, cheese, garlic, sugar, and salt. Shake well to blend thoroughly.

2 The dressing will keep in the refrigerator for up to 2 weeks. Shake well before serving.

This dressing can be made DIABETIC-FRIENDLY by substituting a pinch of stevia for the sugar. Note that you only need a pinch, as stevia is about 300 times sweeter than sugar.

CREAMY CHIPOTLE RANCH
Dressing

GLUTEN-FREE

DIABETIC-FRIENDLY

VEGETARIAN!

Sandy's nephews, John and David, have called this spicy version of ranch dressing "gravy" since they were very small boys, and they add that gravy to just about anything! They not only put it on their salads, they also use it as a dip for raw veggies, as a dip for their pizza, and as a sauce on their mom's fish tacos. The chipotle peppers bring the heat, and the mayo can easily be replaced with plain nonfat yogurt if you want to cut some calories! That is the beauty of making your own dressing—you're in control of your ingredients! *Makes 2 cups*

½ cup mayonnaise

½ cup buttermilk

2 chipotle peppers in adobo sauce, minced

4 garlic cloves, minced

¼ cup chopped fresh cilantro leaves

1 teaspoon salt

1 In a blender, combine the mayonnaise, buttermilk, peppers, garlic, cilantro, and salt. Pulse until the dressing is smooth. If you prefer a chunkier dressing, you can combine the ingredients in a jar with a tight-fitting lid and shake well.

2 The dressing will keep in the refrigerator for up to 2 weeks. Shake well before serving.

FIESTA FRENCH
Dressing

The tanginess of the mustard and vinegar makes this dressing a zesty addition to sandwiches or for perking up a simple green salad. In fact, this dressing is so lively, it's like having a fiesta of flavors in your mouth! When we created this recipe, we found that corn oil worked best. It lends a nice, smooth flavor to the dressing. *Makes 1 cup*

GLUTEN-FREE
VEGETARIAN!

¾ cup corn oil (you can also use olive oil)

¼ cup cider vinegar

2 teaspoons mustard

2 teaspoons paprika

1 teaspoon sugar

2 teaspoons salt

¼ teaspoon freshly ground black pepper

1 In a blender or food processor, combine the oil, vinegar, mustard, paprika, sugar, salt, and pepper. Blend until well combined.

2 The dressing will keep in the refrigerator for up to 2 weeks. Shake well before serving.

This dressing can be made DIABETIC-FRIENDLY by substituting a pinch of stevia for the sugar. Note that you only need a pinch, as stevia is about 300 times sweeter than sugar.

THOUSAND ISLAND
Dressing

Sandy's dad, Max, is a huge fan of this traditional Thousand Island dressing. Much like his grandsons and their "gravy" (see page 118), he dips everything in it. His favorite use for this dressing is for dipping his fries! When Crystal lived in Utah, she saw that restaurants made a similar dressing, which they called "fry sauce." *Makes 1 cup*

GLUTEN-FREE

VEGETARIAN!

1/2 cup mayonnaise

2 tablespoons ketchup

1 tablespoon Heinz chili sauce

1/2 teaspoon Worcestershire sauce

1 tablespoon finely chopped onion

2 teaspoons sweet pickle relish

1 tablespoon sugar

1/2 teaspoon garlic powder

1/4 teaspoon salt

1/8 teaspoon freshly ground black pepper

1 In a large bowl, combine the mayonnaise, ketchup, chili sauce, Worcestershire sauce, onion, relish, sugar, garlic powder, salt, and pepper. Whisk well.

2 Chill in the refrigerator for at least 30 minutes to allow the flavors to combine. Store in an airtight container for up to 2 weeks. Whisk well before serving.

Do you know where the name Thousand Island dressing comes from? It was named after a large cluster of islands (over 1,800 of them) that are scattered on the northern part of Lake Ontario and along the Saint Lawrence River. Once controlled by pirates and bootleggers, the islands later became a popular vacation destination for the rich and famous. While we know the dressing was named for the place where it was created, the origin of the dressing itself is a little more controversial. There are two main stories about the formulation of this popular condiment.

One version states that it was created on the yacht belonging to George Boldt, the proprietor of New York City's Waldorf-Astoria Hotel. According to legend, a resourceful steward mixed it up when he realized that none of the usual ingredients for salad dressing were aboard the yacht. Boldt so enjoyed its distinctive taste that he named it after the area in which they were traveling and added it to the menu at the restaurant of the famed hotel.

The other version is that Sophia LaLonde, the wife of a Thousand Islands fishing guide, came up with the dressing and served it to visiting fishermen who went on excursions led by her husband. When visiting vaudeville star May Irwin tried the dressing, she was so impressed that she asked for the recipe. Mrs. LaLonde shared it with her, as well as with the Herald House, where Miss Irwin was staying, and they, too, began serving it to the public. Miss Irwin named the dressing after her vacation spot and claimed to have later shared the recipe with George Boldt so that he could add it to the menu of the Waldorf-Astoria.

To this day, nobody knows which (if either) of these stories is true. But whether you're Team Boldt or Team LaLonde, we can all agree that this ingenious creation changed salad dressing forever.

BALSAMIC
Vinaigrette

GLUTEN-FREE
DIABETIC-FRIENDLY
VEGETARIAN!

Crystal's go-to favorite, Balsamic Vinaigrette, is low in fat and quite versatile. When drizzled over ripe garden tomatoes, fresh mozzarella, and basil, you have the summer's best salad. This dressing also makes a sweet marinade for grilled chicken breast or pork tenderloin. Crystal especially likes this with our Savory French Onion Tart (page 108). *Makes 2/3 cup*

¼ cup balsamic vinegar

1 tablespoon Dijon mustard

1 garlic clove, minced

6 tablespoons olive oil

1 teaspoon salt

½ teaspoon freshly ground black pepper

1 In a small bowl, whisk together the balsamic vinegar, mustard, and garlic. Add the oil in a slow, steady stream, whisking constantly until well blended. Season with salt and pepper.

2 Store in an airtight container in the refrigerator for up to 2 weeks. Whisk well before serving.

GREEK
Dressing

This delicious and mildly tart dressing is amazing served over a Greek-style salad of lettuce, tomatoes, Kalamata olives, and feta cheese. It's also delicious in a sandwich wrap and even over pasta. Much like the Balsamic Vinaigrette (opposite), this makes a great marinade for chicken and fish, too.

Makes 1 cup

½ cup extra-virgin olive oil

5 tablespoons red wine vinegar

2 tablespoons fresh lemon juice

1½ teaspoons Dijon mustard

2 garlic cloves, minced

¼ teaspoon sugar

1 teaspoon dried oregano

¼ teaspoon salt

1 In a medium bowl, whisk together the olive oil, vinegar, lemon juice, mustard, garlic, sugar, oregano, and salt. Whisk well to blend thoroughly.

2 Store in an airtight container in the refrigerator for up to 2 weeks. Whisk well before serving.

This dressing can be made DIABETIC-FRIENDLY by substituting a pinch of stevia for the sugar. Note that you only need a pinch, as stevia is about 300 times sweeter than sugar.

CRYSTAL'S WEDGE SALAD with
Bacon and Blue Cheese Dressing

Crystal *loves* a wedge salad. When we were on tour for our first book, we'd get back to the hotel some nights completely pooped and starving, and all she wanted was a big wedge salad. A wedge salad may seem like an odd choice, but Crystal is on a personal mission to bring iceberg back! The sometimes-forgotten lettuce can be quite masterful in this setting. The ingredient list is small, but the textures and flavors really pack a punch. From the chilled crispness of the iceberg to the creamy tang of the blue cheese dressing—it is simply divine. Personally, we think the secret to a well-crafted wedge is that each serving should have a density conducive to eating it with a fork and knife. We kept our recipe straightforward, but feel free to top off your creation with crumbled bacon, chopped cherry tomatoes, hard-boiled egg, candied pecans, and even more blue cheese, of course. *Serves 8*

 DIABETIC-FRIENDLY

1 cup mayonnaise

1 (8-ounce) container sour cream

2 tablespoons Worcestershire sauce

2 teaspoons fresh lemon juice

1 cup crumbled blue cheese (4 ounces)

12 slices bacon, cooked and crumbled

1/2 cup shredded Parmesan cheese (2 ounces)

1 garlic clove, minced

1 teaspoon salt

1/2 teaspoon freshly ground black pepper

1 head iceberg lettuce, cut into 8 wedges

1 In a medium bowl, combine the mayonnaise, sour cream, Worcestershire sauce, lemon juice, blue cheese, bacon, Parmesan cheese, garlic, salt, and pepper. Stir well.

2 Put the lettuce wedges on 8 plates. Drizzle 1/4 cup of the dressing over each wedge and serve.

This dish is GLUTEN-FREE as long as your Worcestershire sauce is a gluten-free brand.

TOMATO AND FETA
Salad

Tomato salads are a fresh addition to any meal. This particular salad has a Mediter-

GLUTEN-FREE

DIABETIC-FRIENDLY

VEGETARIAN!

ranean flair, which makes it the perfect accompaniment to a white, flaky fish dish or our Moussaka (page 54). But with a few simple ingredient swaps, the tomato salad can take on an entirely different flavor. Check out our Pint-Size Caprese Salad (page 126) and our Tomato and Avocado Salad (page 127), which lend flavors to complement some of our Italian and Mexican casseroles. Who knew the tomato was so well traveled? *Serves 8*

1 pound ripe plum tomatoes, chopped

1 cucumber, seeded and chopped

1/2 teaspoon oregano

1 cup feta cheese, drained and cut into cubes (8 ounces)

1/2 cup pitted Kalamata olives, chopped

Juice of 1/2 lemon

1/4 cup extra-virgin olive oil

1 teaspoon salt

1/2 teaspoon freshly ground black pepper

8 basil leaves, torn into pieces

In a large bowl, combine the tomatoes, cucumber, oregano, cheese, and olives. Add the lemon juice, oil, salt, and pepper, and toss. Add the basil, toss again, and serve.

PINT-SIZE CAPRESE
Salad

This petite variation of the classic Caprese calls for cherry tomatoes and bocconcini (bite-size fresh mozzarella balls), but don't let the pint-size ingredients fool you—they pack the same flavorful punch. The flavors are brightened here with lemon juice and fresh basil, while the balsamic vinegar adds acidity. Serve with red pepper flakes on the side if you want to spice things up even more! *Serves 6*

GLUTEN-FREE

DIABETIC-FRIENDLY

VEGETARIAN!

1 tablespoon lemon juice

1 cup fresh basil leaves (about 20), plus a few for garnish

1 small clove garlic, minced

1/3 cup extra-virgin olive oil

1 pint cherry tomatoes, halved

1 cup bocconcini, drained and halved

1/2 teaspoon salt

1/4 teaspoon freshly ground black pepper

2 tablespoons aged balsamic vinegar

1 In a food processor or blender, blend together the lemon juice, basil, and garlic. With the machine running, gradually pour in the olive oil, blending to form a smooth dressing.

2 Pour the dressing into a medium bowl and add the tomatoes and cheese. Season with the salt and pepper, and toss well. Garnish with a few torn basil leaves and the balsamic vinegar.

TOMATO AND AVOCADO
Salad

When making a salad, sometimes less is more. The undeniable stars of this simple salad are the tomato and the avocado, and in our opinion, this may be one of the best-tasting combinations that nature has ever produced! Try this salad with a Mexican dish, as its clean flavors balance out the spice and heavy cheese most Mexican recipes call for. It pairs especially well with our Chicken Enchiladas (page 68) and Yvonne's Unstuffed Poblano Casserole (page 58). *Serves 6*

GLUTEN-FREE

DIABETIC-FRIENDLY

VEGETARIAN!

2 Roma tomatoes, chopped

1 avocado, chopped

1 red onion, sliced

2 tablespoons fresh lemon juice

1/2 teaspoon salt

1/4 teaspoon freshly ground black pepper

10 fresh cilantro leaves, for garnish

Put the tomatoes and the avocado in a medium bowl. Add the onion, lemon juice, salt, and pepper, and toss well. Garnish with the cilantro and serve.

JAYNE'S MARINATED
Vegetable Salad

This salad always reminds Sandy and her husband, Michael, of his family gatherings in his parents' backyard. Everyone is lounging around by the pool sipping cocktails and watching Michael's dad, Mike, prepare the grill. On warm Austin days, nothing is as refreshing as Jayne's (Michael's mom) marinated salad. It is cool, crisp, and has the perfect amount of crunch. Since it is best made beforehand and chilled overnight, you, too, can look like Jayne, the effortlessly fabulous hostess. Kick back with a glass of wine before guests arrive—the salad is ready! *Serves 10*

GLUTEN-FREE

VEGETARIAN!

1 cup cider vinegar

¾ cup sugar

½ cup vegetable oil

1 (11-ounce) can shoepeg corn, drained

1 (9-ounce) box frozen baby peas, thawed and drained

1 (14.5-ounce) can French-style green beans, drained

½ onion, chopped

2 celery ribs, chopped

1 green bell pepper, chopped

1 (4-ounce) jar pimentos, chopped, drained

1 teaspoon salt

½ teaspoon freshly ground black pepper

1 In a small saucepan set over medium-high heat, bring the vinegar to a boil. Add the sugar, reduce the heat to medium, and simmer for 5 minutes, until the sugar is dissolved. Remove the pan from the heat and add the oil.

2 In a large bowl, combine the corn, peas, green beans, onion, celery, green pepper, pimentos, salt, and pepper. Pour the vinegar mixture over the vegetables. Chill the salad for 8 hours or overnight. Serve cold.

This recipe can be made DIABETIC-FRIENDLY by substituting garbanzo beans for the corn. Diabetics need to be mindful of corn because of its high sugar content. Also, substitute a pinch of stevia for the sugar. Note that you only need a pinch, as stevia is about 300 times sweeter than sugar.

CHICKEN
ENCHILADAS
page 68

TOMATO AND
AVOCADO SALAD
page 127

TATER TOT
CASSEROLE
page 110

CIOPPINO-STYLE
ROASTED CRAB
page 63

BRUSSELS SPROUTS WITH
BACON, GARLIC, AND SHALLOTS
page 146

BAKED SAUSAGES WITH FENNEL
page 48

SHRIMP GUMBO CASSEROLE
page 44

HARGILL'S BUNCO
CLUB 7-LAYER SALAD
page 129

DILL BREAD
page 160

CHEESY
GRITS-STUFFED
EGGPLANT
ROLLS WITH
TOMATO SAUCE
page 82

GREEN CHILI AND
CHICKEN BAKE
page 96

**SUPER-SIMPLE
SPINACH-STUFFED
SHELLS**
page 100

CHICKEN WITH
40 CLOVES OF GARLIC
page 43

CARROT SOUFFLÉ
page 150

ASPARAGUS BUNDLES
WRAPPED IN PROSCIUTTO
page 143

AWESOME AUSSIE
MEAT PIES
page 70

BBQ PORK RIBS
page 37

CRYSTAL'S MAY-I-HAVE-
MORE-MAYO POTATO SALAD
page 130

ZUCCHINI LASAGNA
page 76

BROCCOLI SALAD
page 133

**AUNT FANNIE'S CABIN
SQUASH CASSEROLE**
page 148

**ROSEMARY
BAKED HAM**
page 78

KEY WEST
CLAFOUTI
page 164

GRANNY HALEY'S ANGEL
FOOD CAKE WITH VANILLA
STRAWBERRY SAUCE
page 172

S'MORE PIE
page 176

HARGILL'S BUNCO CLUB
7-Layer Salad

My, oh my, this is a Hargill, Texas, classic recipe. This seven-layer salad has made an appearance at pretty much every Bunco party, church supper, baby shower, picnic, and family reunion Sandy can think of. Sealing the top of the salad with mayo is the key to its freshness and creaminess. Give it a try. It will be a favorite for your family, too! *Serves 10*

GLUTEN-FREE

2 cups spring salad mix

1 bunch green onions, green parts only, chopped

1 green bell pepper, chopped

1 (16-ounce) bag frozen peas

2 cups mayonnaise

1 tablespoon sugar

2 cups shredded sharp Cheddar cheese (8 ounces)

12 slices bacon, cooked and crumbled

1 In a 9 x13-inch casserole dish, layer the salad in this order: spring salad mix, green onions, green bell peppers, and frozen peas.

2 In a small bowl, combine the mayonnaise and the sugar. Spread the mayonnaise over the top of the veggies, completely sealing in the goodies below. Top the mayonnaise with the cheese and the bacon. Chill in the refrigerator for 1 hour before serving.

This recipe can be made DIABETIC-FRIENDLY by substituting a pinch of stevia for the sugar. Note that you only need a pinch, as stevia is about 300 times sweeter than sugar.

CRYSTAL'S MAY-I-HAVE-MORE-MAYO
Potato Salad

Potato salad is like wine in that it is very much about personal taste. Some like a

GLUTEN-FREE

VEGETARIAN!

mustard-based salad, some like a mayo-based one, and some like a combination of both. For Crystal, it has to be mayo, and she likes to add a little Greek yogurt for some tang. Mixed up with tons of fresh herbs, this potato salad is amazingly light and refreshing! Make it ahead of time, 'cause again (like wine), it is better after it has aged. *Serves 8*

3 pounds red potatoes

1 teaspoon salt

1/2 teaspoon freshly ground black pepper

1/2 cup mayonnaise

1/2 cup Greek yogurt

3 tablespoons rice vinegar

3 green onions, green parts only, thinly sliced

3 celery ribs, chopped

1/2 cup chopped fresh parsley

1/2 cup chopped fresh basil

3 tablespoons chopped fresh dill

2 teaspoons finely grated lemon zest

1 **Put the potatoes in a large pot of heavily salted water. Bring to a boil, reduce the heat to medium-low, and simmer until the potatoes are tender, about 17 minutes. Drain and let cool.**

2 **Cut potatoes into 3/4-inch pieces, put them in a large bowl, and season with the salt and pepper. In a separate bowl, combine the mayonnaise, yogurt, and vinegar, and pour the mixture over the potatoes. Add the green onions, celery, parsley, basil, dill, and lemon zest, and toss well. Cover and refrigerate overnight before serving (if you can wait that long). The salad will keep in the refrigerator for up to 5 days.**

COMMUNITY-BUILDING
Warm Bacon Spinach Salad

Hargill—the town where Sandy grew up—is not large by any means. There is a single community building in town where folks hold family reunions, the annual Hargill cook-off, and many wedding celebrations. At the center of most events is a potluck dinner, and this salad is a community staple and almost always makes an appearance. This salad simply bursts with flavor, most notably from the bacon, as well as the great balance of the sweet sautéed onions and tangy vinegar. Delish! *Serves 8*

¼ cup olive oil

1 medium onion, thinly sliced

1 tablespoon all-purpose flour

1 tablespoon sugar

1 teaspoon dry mustard

¼ cup sherry vinegar

1 teaspoon salt

½ teaspoon freshly ground black pepper

1 (10-ounce) bag fresh spinach

3 slices bacon, cooked and crumbled

1 large hard-boiled egg, sliced

2 cups croutons

1 In a medium skillet set over medium-high heat, add the oil and onion and cook until the onion begins to soften, about 6 minutes.

2 In a small bowl, combine the flour, sugar, and dry mustard. Add the mixture to the onion mixture. Gradually add the vinegar and 1 cup of water to the pan and cook, stirring constantly, until thickened, about 5 minutes. Season with the salt and pepper.

3 Divide the spinach among 8 plates. Pour the warm dressing over the spinach and garnish with the crumbled bacon, egg slices, and croutons.

This dish can be made GLUTEN-FREE by replacing the flour with a gluten-free all-purpose mix, either store bought (see page 15 for recommendations of our favorite brands) or homemade (see page 186 for our recipe), and using gluten-free croutons.

This recipe can be made DIABETIC-FRIENDLY by substituting a pinch of stevia for the sugar. Note that you only need a pinch, as stevia is about 300 times sweeter than sugar.

JAYNE'S SEAFOOD
Pasta Salad

Sandy's mother-in-law, Jayne, is one of our favorite people in the world. You would be hard pressed to find someone kinder and more supportive than she is. This recipe is her specialty, and she is given much grief if a family event comes and goes without its appearance. Do yourself a favor and make it today! *Serves 4 to 6*

1 (8-ounce) package orecchiette pasta

2 tablespoons olive oil

6 large hard-boiled eggs, chopped

1 cup mayonnaise

1/3 cup Heinz chili sauce

1/4 cup sour cream

1 tablespoon fresh lemon juice

1 1/2 teaspoons salt

12 ounces crabmeat

2 pounds fresh shrimp, boiled, chilled, peeled, and deveined

1 celery rib, chopped

1/2 cup chopped broccoli, lightly steamed

1/4 cup sliced green onions, green parts only

1 In a large pot of boiling salted water, cook the pasta until al dente, about 12 minutes. Drain and rinse the pasta under cold water. Put the pasta in a large bowl, add the olive oil, and toss to coat. Cover the bowl and chill in the refrigerator for at least 1 hour.

2 In another large bowl, combine the eggs, mayonnaise, chili sauce, sour cream, lemon juice, and salt, and mix well. Add the crabmeat, shrimp, celery, broccoli, and green onions, and stir well. Cover the bowl and chill for at least 3 hours.

3 Add the chilled pasta to the crabmeat mixture and mix well. The salad will keep in the refrigerator for up to 3 days.

This dish can be made GLUTEN-FREE by using a gluten-free pasta. See page 15 for recommendations of our favorite brands.

There is enough protein in this recipe to make the dish DIABETIC-FRIENDLY, as long as you replace the orecchiette with a whole-wheat pasta that is high in fiber.

BROCCOLI SALAD

You'll be surprised how this tasty salad tricks many picky eaters into dining on

veggies! Crystal's sister-in-law Ramona employs this salad to get her daughter Chloe to eat her broccoli. The trick lies in the combination of the flavors—the raw broccoli pairs beautifully with salty bacon and a sweet and creamy dressing.

Serves 8

6 cups fresh broccoli florets, chopped

8 slices bacon, cooked and crumbled

3 green onions, green parts only, chopped

1/2 cup dried cranberries or raisins

1/2 cup chopped pecans

1 cup mayonnaise

2 tablespoons cider vinegar

1/2 cup sugar

1 In a large bowl, combine the broccoli, bacon, green onions, cranberries, and pecans.

2 In a separate bowl, combine the mayonnaise, vinegar, and sugar to make a dressing. Pour the dressing over the broccoli mixture and toss well. Serve room temperature or cold.

This dish can be made DIABETIC-FRIENDLY by omitting the dried fruit and substituting a sugar substitute like stevia for the sugar. Take a look at the guidelines on the sweetener package to know how much to put in the salad, since something like Splenda is much sweeter than sugar.

PANZANELLA
Salad

VEGETARIAN!

If you've ever tried traditional panzanella, then you know it's basically a bread salad made with lots of fresh vegetables. Our version includes the usual tomatoes and basil, along with cucumbers for crunch, Kalamata olives for a little salty goodness, and some creamy fontina cheese, because cheese makes everything even better! This is a great summer salad to bring to a cookout. *Serves 8*

6 cups day-old Italian bread, torn into bite-size pieces

1/3 cup plus 3 tablespoons olive oil

3 garlic cloves, minced

2 teaspoons salt

1 teaspoon freshly ground black pepper

1/4 cup fresh lemon juice

2 tablespoons red wine vinegar

1 teaspoon sugar

4 Roma tomatoes, chopped

1 cucumber, seeded and chopped

1 cup cubed fontina cheese (4 ounces)

1/2 cup Kalamata olives, pitted and halved

10 fresh basil leaves, shredded

1 Preheat the oven to 400°F.

2 On a baking sheet, toss the bread with 1/3 cup of the oil, the garlic, 1/2 teaspoon of the salt, and 1/4 teaspoon of the pepper. Spread into a single layer and bake for 5 to 10 minutes, or until crispy, stirring a few times to ensure that it toasts evenly.

3 In a small bowl, whisk together the lemon juice, vinegar, sugar, 1 teaspoon of the salt, and 1/2 teaspoon of the pepper. Drizzle in the remaining 3 tablespoons of oil, whisking until blended.

4 In a bowl, toss the toasted bread with the tomatoes, cucumber, cheese, olives, and basil. Drizzle with the dressing and season with the remaining 1/2 teaspoon of salt and the remaining 1/4 teaspoon pepper. Let sit for 10 minutes before serving.

This recipe can be made GLUTEN-FREE by using a gluten-free bread. See page 15 for recommendations of our favorite brands.

CORNBREAD SALAD TWO WAYS

Even though we Queens grew up in different states, we have eerily similar lives—so similar, in fact, that we are still trying to figure out how we're related. Both of us come from large families with parents who have been married over fifty years; both have four siblings; both are the youngest child. Crystal's mother's middle name is Irene; Sandy had a grandmother named Irene. We even have the same birthday. But most important, we grew up eating similar foods, but with regional twists. Here is the Pollock version of Cornbread Salad, and the Cook version follows. *Serves 6*

5 cups crumbled Mexican Cornbread (page 190)

1 pound bacon, cooked and crumbled

1 red bell pepper, seeded and chopped

1 cucumber, seeded and chopped

2 large beefsteak tomatoes, diced

1 bunch green onions, green parts only, sliced

1 cup Creamy Chipotle Ranch Dressing (page 118), or store-bought ranch dressing

1 In a large bowl, combine the cornbread, bacon, red bell pepper, cucumber, tomatoes, and green onions.

2 Pour the salad dressing over the salad and toss to coat. Serve immediately.

Cook Family Version
SERVES 6

1 recipe Cook's Cornbread, crumbled (page 191)

2 (15.5-ounce) cans pinto beans, rinsed and drained

1 onion, chopped

1 green bell pepper, seeded and chopped

1 beefsteak tomato, chopped

1 cup mayonnaise

1/2 cup sweet gherkins pickle juice

1 pound bacon, cooked and crumbled

In a 9 x 13-inch casserole dish, layer the ingredients as follows: cornbread, beans, onion, bell pepper, tomato, mayo, pickle juice, and bacon. Cover and chill overnight. Serve cold.

These dishes can be made GLUTEN-FREE if you use a gluten-free cornbread mix to make your cornbread. We recommend Bob's Red Mill Gluten Free Cornbread Mix.

A FEW OF SANDY'S FAVORITE THINGS
Orzo Pasta Salad

 **VEGETARIAN!**

Pasta tossed with peppery arugula and leeks (yum!)
Engagement and marriage to computer geeks (just one!)
Memories like these carry my mind to Spring
'Cause these are a few of my favorite things

When the dog bites! (never a pug, they are angels)
When the bee stings (bastard!)
When I'm feeling sad (out of wine)
I simply remember (to eat) my favorite things
And then I don't feel so bad!!!!! ('nuff said!)

Serves 8

1 pound orzo pasta

1 teaspoon salt plus more
for pasta water

2 garlic cloves, minced

1 teaspoon olive oil

1 leek, white and pale green
parts only, thinly sliced

1 cup baby arugula

1½ cups pine nuts

Juice of 1 lemon

1 teaspoon salt

½ teaspoon freshly ground
black pepper

1 cup grated Parmesan
cheese (4 ounces)

1 In a medium saucepan set over high heat, cook the orzo in boiling salted water until tender, about 10 minutes. Drain the pasta and set aside to cool.

2 In a small saucepan set over medium-high heat, sauté the garlic in the olive oil. Add the leeks and 1 teaspoon salt, and cook for about 3 minutes. Stir in the arugula and cook until wilted, about 3 minutes.

3 Put the orzo in a medium bowl and add the pine nuts, lemon juice, salt, and pepper. Toss well. Sprinkle the cheese over the top of the salad. Serve warm or cold.

This recipe can be made GLUTEN-FREE by substituting quinoa for the orzo.

TOMATO, GOAT CHEESE,
and Quinoa Salad

This warm quinoa salad makes a powerful sidekick for any entrée. It has a similar texture to that of couscous or rice, with a slight crunch and a somewhat nutty flavor. Quinoa is considered a superfood because it contains more protein than any other grain. And this protein is complete, containing all nine essential amino acids—talk about a boost! Mix it with tomato and garlic and goat cheese for a delicious dish that packs quite a nutritional punch. *Serves 6 to 8*

GLUTEN-FREE

DIABETIC-FRIENDLY

VEGETARIAN!

1 cup quinoa

1 teaspoon salt

2 tablespoons olive oil

2 garlic cloves, minced

¼ cup balsamic vinegar

1 pint cherry tomatoes, halved

1 (5.3-ounce) container goat cheese, crumbled

½ cup fresh basil, thinly sliced, plus more for garnish

1 Put the quinoa in a strainer and rinse it under warm water until the water runs clear.

2 Bring 3 cups of water and the salt to a boil in a medium saucepan. Add the quinoa and bring it back to a boil. Reduce the heat to low, cover the pan, and simmer for 15 minutes, or until the quinoa is tender and translucent. Drain off the water and put the quinoa in a bowl.

3 Heat the olive oil in a medium sauté pan set over medium-high heat. Add the garlic and cook for 1 minute. Add the balsamic vinegar and tomatoes and toss to coat.

4 Cook, stirring occasionally, until the mixture has reduced and become syrupy, 15 to 20 minutes. Pour the tomato mixture into the bowl of quinoa and toss to mix. Add the goat cheese and basil and toss well. Garnish with more basil and serve warm.

SASSY
SIDES

Side Dishes
with Attitude

It's nice to get a compliment on your dish—but how about a side to "complement" it even more? You may want to put a bookmark in this chapter, because it's all about creating the perfect partners for our main casseroles. And get ready—we're going to rock your world, as most of our sides break out of the 9 x 13-inch mold! This chapter will help you find innovative ways to elevate your favorite vegetables and put the finishing touches to your family meal, holiday ham, or dinner party. "Why, what a lovely side dish you have there!" Ding!

- **SPINACH AND SPICE AND EVERYTHING NICE**

- **MAMAW'S POTATO CASSEROLE**

- **BROCCOLI RABE WITH SHALLOTS**

- **ASPARAGUS BUNDLES WRAPPED IN PROSCIUTTO**

- **CORN PUDDING**

- **BRUSSELS SPROUTS WITH BACON, GARLIC, AND SHALLOTS**

- **BRAISED ENDIVE GRATIN**

- **AUNT FANNIE'S CABIN SQUASH CASSEROLE**

- **CARROT SOUFFLÉ**

- **RISOTTO WITH ASPARAGUS AND LEMON**

- **NENE'S SPANISH RICE**

- **ROYAL RATATOUILLE**

- **WILD RICE**

- **SIMPLE HERB-ROASTED VEGETABLES**

- **CURRIED RICE VEGGIE BAKE**

- **DILL BREAD**

- **POTATOES TWO TIMES WITH A KICK CASSEROLE**

SPINACH AND SPICE
and Everything Nice

GLUTEN-FREE

DIABETIC-FRIENDLY

VEGETARIAN!

The spiciness of this dish comes from pickled jalapeños. Sandy always has pickled jalapeños in her fridge, and they are perhaps her favorite condiment. She will add them to sandwiches, eggs, tacos, quesadillas . . . you name it! In fact, she would never dream of letting a single jalapeño go to waste. She even uses the pickling liquid to flavor stir-fries and veggies. Spinach prepared the way we do here makes a nice side for our BBQ Pork Ribs (page 37) and Chicken Paprikash (page 72). Crystal prefers to leave out the jalapeños, adding a little more lemon juice instead to brighten it up. Prepared that way, it pairs nicely with dishes such as our Gnocchi Bake (page 66). *Serves 6 to 8*

3 tablespoons olive oil

¼ cup chopped pickled jalapeños (about 20 slices)

4 garlic cloves, minced

1 pound fresh spinach

¼ cup pickled jalapeño juice (from the jar)

2 tablespoons fresh lemon juice

¼ teaspoon salt

¼ teaspoon freshly ground black pepper

1 In a sauté pan set over medium heat, heat the olive oil.

2 Add the jalapeños and garlic and cook for about 2 minutes, or until the garlic just begins to brown.

3 Add the spinach and sauté for 2 minutes.

4 Add the jalapeño juice, lemon juice, salt, and pepper, and stir well. Serve hot.

MAMAW'S POTATO CASSEROLE

Simple ingredients and preparation, but always warm and comforting, this is just one of those dishes that reminds you of home. Crystal stayed with her mamaw Cook often when growing up, and Mamaw always served this dish alongside a variety of entrées. Maybe it was because she always had the dish's affordable and readily available staples on hand, or maybe it was because it tasted so good. Either way, it makes quite a satisfying meal when paired with a roasted chicken (page 200) and a simple side dish like our Spinach and Spice and Everything Nice (opposite). *Serves 6*

Cooking spray

2 russet potatoes, peeled and thinly sliced

1 teaspoon salt

1/2 teaspoon freshly ground black pepper

1 (10 3/4-ounce) can of cream of chicken soup, or 1 1/2 cups homemade (page 196)

1/2 cup evaporated milk

1 medium onion, thinly sliced

1/4 cup (1/2 stick) unsalted butter, cut into small pieces

1 Preheat the oven to 350°F. Spray a 9 x 13-inch casserole dish with cooking spray.

2 Put the potatoes in the prepared casserole dish, season with the salt and pepper, and toss well.

3 In a large bowl, combine the soup, evaporated milk, and 1/3 cup water. Pour the mixture over the potatoes. Lay the onion slices on top of the casserole and dot with the butter.

4 Bake for 1 hour, until potatoes are fork-tender.

FREEZES WELL! For best results, prepare the casserole through step 3. Wrap in foil and freeze for up to 2 months. Thaw the casserole overnight in the refrigerator before baking as stated in the recipe. Note that casseroles that have not been completely thawed may take 15 to 30 minutes longer, so be sure to check for bubbling edges and a hot center.

This dish is GLUTEN-FREE as long as the cream of chicken soup is gluten-free. See page 196 for our recipe or page 15 for recommendations of our favorite brands.

BROCCOLI RABE
with Shallots

GLUTEN-FREE

DIABETIC-FRIENDLY

VEGETARIAN!

Broccoli Rabe (think "Rob" when you say it, not "babe"!) is made up of long, leafy greens with small broccoli-like florets. Although broccoli and broccoli rabe are similarly named and are both rich in vitamins and nutrients, the two vegetables are pretty different. The biggest difference is how they taste. Broccoli rabe is slightly bitter, so we suggest that you blanch it first before you sauté it in the yummy shallot-infused oil. Pair it with our Super-Simple Spinach-Stuffed Shells (page 100) to impress your guests! They will never know that dinner came together in such a flash. *Serves 6 to 8*

2 bunches broccoli rabe

2 tablespoons extra-virgin olive oil

4 medium shallots, minced

1 teaspoon salt

½ teaspoon red pepper flakes

1 Trim the ends off the broccoli rabe. Bring a large pot of salted water to a rapid boil over high heat. Add the broccoli rabe and cook for about 3 minutes. Use a slotted spoon to transfer the broccoli rabe to a large bowl of ice-cold water to stop the cooking. When completely cold, drain it well.

2 Heat the oil in a 12-inch nonstick skillet set over moderate heat. Add the shallots and cook, stirring occasionally, until they have browned slightly, about 5 minutes. Add the broccoli rabe and cook for 8 to 10 minutes, or until the broccoli rabe starts to brown. Season with the salt and red pepper flakes. Serve warm.

ASPARAGUS BUNDLES
Wrapped in Prosciutto

This delicious side dish makes an appearance at Crystal's sister Cindy's holiday table every year. There is just something so elegant about the presentation of the neatly wrapped bundles. Crystal and her sister prefer the texture of the whipped cream cheese because it makes it much easier to fold in the herbs and spread the cheese onto the prosciutto without tearing it. If you can't find whipped cream cheese, regular will do—just let it soften before adding the garlic and herbs. Crystal and her sister also prefer the taste of prosciutto, but you can easily substitute pancetta if need be. *Serves 8*

GLUTEN-FREE

DIABETIC-FRIENDLY

Cooking spray

1 (8-ounce) package whipped cream cheese, at room temperature

3 garlic gloves, minced

3 tablespoons finely chopped fresh chives

1 tablespoon finely chopped fresh flat-leaf parsley

1/2 teaspoon salt

1/4 teaspoon freshly ground black pepper

3 pounds asparagus spears, trimmed to 4- to 5-inch-long tips

Extra-virgin olive oil, for drizzling

8 slices prosciutto

1 Preheat the oven to 400°F. Spray a slotted broiler pan with cooking spray.

2 In a medium bowl, combine the cream cheese, garlic, 2 tablespoons of the chives, and the parsley, salt, and pepper, and stir well. Set aside.

3 Lightly coat asparagus spears in the oil. Divide the asparagus into 8 piles. Take a slice of prosciutto and spread a thin layer of the cream cheese mixture on one side. Take one pile of asparagus and put it on a short end of the prosciutto. Roll the asparagus up in the prosciutto and set the bundle on the prepared broiler pan, seam side down. Repeat with the remaining ingredients.

4 Bake for 10 to 12 minutes, until the asparagus is crisp-tender and the prosciutto has browned. Put on a serving dish and garnish with the remaining 1 tablespoon of chives. Serve warm.

CORN PUDDING

Summers wouldn't be complete without fresh, sweet corn! When Crystal first moved to Austin, Sandy introduced her to a type of Mexican street food that very well may

VEGETARIAN!

have changed the way she viewed life: gigantic ears of roasted corn smothered in Mexican crema and sprinkled with lots of spice and lime juice. They call it *elote*, but we call it delish! It is the perfect treat, the sweetness of the corn blending so perfectly with the southwestern spices.

Another one of our favorite ways to enjoy summer corn is in this pudding. Our love of *elote* made us realize that this sweet, velvety dish is an ideal match for some of our spicier fare. Try serving it with Yvonne's Unstuffed Poblano Casserole (page 58) for a real fiesta! *Serves 6 to 8*

Cooking spray

2 tablespoons olive oil

½ green bell pepper, finely chopped

1 small onion, finely chopped

1 tablespoon all-purpose flour

1 (16-ounce) can creamed corn

1 cup bread crumbs, homemade (page 188) or store bought

1 cup whole milk

1 large egg

1 teaspoon salt

1 Preheat the oven to 350°F. Spray a 9 x 13-inch casserole dish with cooking spray.

2 In a large skillet set over medium-high heat, heat the olive oil. Add the bell pepper and onion and cook for 6 minutes, or until they are soft. Add the flour and stir to coat the veggies. Cook for 1 minute more, to cook out the raw-flour taste.

3 In a large bowl, combine the corn, ½ cup of the bread crumbs, the milk, egg, and salt. Add the onion mixture to the bowl and mix well. Pour the mixture into the prepared casserole dish. Sprinkle the remaining ½ cup of bread crumbs on top.

4 Bake for 30 minutes, or until browned and set. Serve hot.

FREEZES WELL! For best results, prepare the casserole through step 3. Wrap in foil and freeze for up to 2 months. Thaw the casserole overnight in the refrigerator before baking as stated in the recipe. Note that casseroles that have not been completely thawed may take 15 to 30 minutes longer, so be sure to check for bubbling edges and a hot center.

This dish can be made GLUTEN-FREE by replacing the flour with a gluten-free all-purpose mix, either store bought (see page 15 for recommendations of our favorite brands) or homemade (see page 186 for our recipe). You can also purchase gluten-free bread crumbs (see page 15 for brands) or make your own (see page 188 for our recipe).

BRUSSELS SPROUTS
with Bacon, Garlic, and Shallots

Brussels sprouts are a food that seldom elicits a cheer from dinner guests. But when

GLUTEN-FREE

DIABETIC-FRIENDLY

you serve them like this, you're gonna get a "Heck, yeah!" Brussels sprouts are pleasingly bitter when sautéed and are perfect for pairing with bacon. Your guests may start doing cartwheels and backflips and try to form themselves into a pyramid. Don't say we didn't warn you! Serve with our Chicken with 40 Cloves of Garlic (page 43). *Serves 8*

6 slices bacon, chopped

1½ pounds Brussels sprouts, trimmed and halved

½ cup sliced shallots (about 1 large)

6 garlic cloves, thinly sliced

¾ cup chicken stock, homemade (see page 192) or store bought

⅛ teaspoon salt

⅛ teaspoon freshly ground black pepper

1 Heat a large nonstick skillet over medium heat. Add the bacon and cook for 5 minutes, or until it begins to brown. Transfer the bacon to a paper towel–lined plate.

2 Increase the heat to medium-high. Add the Brussels sprouts and shallots to the bacon fat and cook for 4 minutes. Add the garlic and cook for 4 more minutes, stirring frequently, or until the garlic begins to brown. Add the chicken stock and bring the mixture to a boil. Cook for 5 minutes, or until the stock mostly evaporates and the sprouts are crisp-tender, stirring occasionally. Remove the pan from the heat. Season with the salt and pepper. Stir in the bacon and serve.

BRAISED ENDIVE GRATIN

Cooking endive in a bit of butter and lemon juice transforms its otherwise crisp and bitter leaves into tender, luscious, almost sweet bundles. This recipe is great as a side dish for our "Like a Good Neighbor" Ham and Gruyère Strata (page 38), as well as just for snacking! Tasty! *Serves 8*

VEGETARIAN!

Cooking spray

¼ cup (½ stick) unsalted butter

3 tablespoons fresh lemon juice

1 tablespoon sugar

½ teaspoon salt

8 endive, cut in half

2 cups bread crumbs, homemade (page 188) or store bought

1 cup shredded Parmesan cheese (4 ounces)

2 tablespoons chopped fresh parsley

1 Preheat the oven to 350°F. Spray a 9 x 13-inch casserole dish with cooking spray.

2 In a large sauté pan set over medium heat, melt 2 tablespoons of the butter. Add the lemon juice, sugar, and salt, and stir well. Put the endive, cut side down, into the butter and cook for 5 minutes. Flip the endive over and cook the second side for 5 minutes, or until the endive start to brown. Put the endive, cut side down, into the prepared casserole dish. Cover the dish and bake for 15 minutes, or until a knife can be easily inserted in the endive.

3 Meanwhile, in a small saucepan set over medium heat, melt the remaining 2 tablespoons of butter. Add the bread crumbs and stir. Pour the bread crumbs into a bowl, add the cheese and parsley, and toss to combine.

4 Remove the dish from the oven and sprinkle the top of the endive with the bread crumb mixture. Return the dish to the oven and bake for 5 more minutes to brown the bread crumbs. Serve hot.

This dish can be made GLUTEN-FREE by using gluten-free bread crumbs, either store bought (see page 15 for recommendations of our favorite brands) or homemade (see page 188 for our recipe).

This recipe can be made DIABETIC-FRIENDLY by substituting a pinch of stevia for the sugar. Note that you only need a pinch, as stevia is about 300 times sweeter than sugar.

AUNT FANNIE'S CABIN
Squash Casserole

Crystal has been fortunate enough to live in the same state as her sister Cindy for quite some time now, while the rest of her family is still in Georgia. So when times are tough and it's difficult to financially swing two back-to-back holiday trips, Crystal is lucky enough to get to have Thanksgiving dinner with her sister. Cindy is an amazing cook, and she allows all her family guests a side dish or dessert request. Crystal always ask for the Asparagus Bundles Wrapped in Prosciutto (page 143); Colin requests pumpkin pie; Keely gets mashed potatoes, sweet potato soufflé, and rolls (apparently she has a lot to be thankful about!); and Kris always asks for this squash casserole. Crystal's aunt Joan got the recipe from one of her favorite restaurants, Aunt Fannie's Cabin, in Smyrna, Georgia. The restaurant is now closed, but its squash casserole lives on. *Serves 6 to 8*

Cooking spray

3 pounds yellow summer squash, chopped

1 small onion, chopped

2 large eggs

½ cup (1 stick) unsalted butter

1 tablespoon sugar

1 teaspoon salt

1 teaspoon freshly ground black pepper

½ cup saltine crackers, crushed

1 Preheat the oven to 375°F. Spray a 9 x 13-inch casserole dish with cooking spray.

2 In a large saucepan set over high heat, combine 3 cups of water and the squash and bring to a boil. Boil until squash is fork-tender, about 15 minutes. Drain the squash in a colander, transfer to a bowl, and mash it with a fork. Add the onion, eggs, ¼ cup of the butter, the sugar, salt, and pepper, and stir well. Pour the mixture into the prepared casserole dish.

3 Melt the remaining ¼ cup of butter and pour it over the top of the casserole. Sprinkle with the crushed crackers. Bake for about 1 hour, or until brown on top. Serve hot.

This dish can be made GLUTEN-FREE by using gluten-free saltines.

This recipe can be made DIABETIC-FRIENDLY by substituting a pinch of stevia for the sugar. Note that you only need a pinch, as stevia is about 300 times sweeter than sugar. You should also replace the saltine cracker topping with a low-carb bread crumb, or simply omit it.

The story around this recipe reminds us that we all have our favorite casseroles and comfort dishes from our childhood. So the next time you plan to have friends over, why not make it a potluck where everyone shares their favorite recipe from their youth? What's interesting about this party idea is that it lets everyone bring something unique to the table. During dinner, guests can explain how their dishes came about and tell any favorite family stories associated with it, such as the Thanksgiving when Aunt Ida pulled out her famous congealed salad from her fridge and it slid across the floor. Extra points go to guests who bring their recipes with them or a special childhood photo from the time during which they typically ate their famed family dish. And the grand prize goes to the story that gets everyone rolling on the floor, just like Aunt Ida's congealed salad!

CARROT SOUFFLÉ

Sandy always makes this savory, light, and airy carrot soufflé at Thanksgiving. The fall season and root vegetables are a natural combination. For a more elegant presentation, try crowning your soufflé. (After all, we are Queens, ya know!) What does that mean, you ask? Soufflés are most impressive when they rise dramatically over the rim of the baking dish. To create this beautiful crown on your own soufflé, fill the dish about three-quarters full. If it's less full, the soufflé may not rise over the rim; if it's more full, the soufflé may spill over unless you wrap the dish with a collar. Make a "collar" on the rim of the dish with a double layer of parchment paper or aluminum foil that extends 3 inches above the dish. If using foil, coat one side of the foil strip generously with melted butter, and wrap the buttered side of the foil around the outside of dish. Tie the collar securely with kitchen twine. *Serves 8*

VEGETARIAN!

Cooking spray

1³⁄₄ pounds carrots, peeled and chopped

1 teaspoon salt

¼ teaspoon freshly ground black pepper

2 tablespoons unsalted butter

2 tablespoons all-purpose flour

½ cup warm milk

½ cup roasted unsalted almonds, finely chopped

4 large eggs, separated

1 Preheat the oven to 350°F. Spray an 8 x 8-inch casserole dish with cooking spray.

2 Put the carrots in a large pot of lightly salted water. Bring to a boil and cook until the carrots are tender, about 20 minutes. Drain and return the carrots to the pot. Add ½ teaspoon of the salt and the pepper. Mash the carrots with a fork or put them through a potato ricer.

3 In a large saucepan set over medium heat, melt the butter. Add the flour and whisk to combine. Gradually add the milk and the remaining ½ teaspoon of salt. Bring to a simmer and cook for 5 minutes, or until slightly thickened. Stir in the carrots and almonds. Remove the pan from the heat. Beat the egg yolks together, then stir them into the carrot mixture. Let cool until the mixture is lukewarm.

4 Meanwhile, beat the egg whites until stiff but not dry, about 4 minutes. Fold the egg whites into the carrot mixture. Gently pour the mixture into the prepared dish. Bake for 50 to 60 minutes, until the soufflé feels firm at the center, or until a sharp knife inserted in the center comes out clean. Serve immediately, scooping out portions with a large spoon.

This dish can be made GLUTEN-FREE by replacing the flour with a gluten-free all-purpose mix, either store bought (see page 15 for recommendations of our favorite brands) or homemade (see page 186 for our recipe).

RISOTTO
with Asparagus and Lemon

Risotto is one of those foods that is very impressive and seems difficult, but the secrets to mastering it are very easy. You just have to pay attention and stir! Paired with savory yet sweet roasted asparagus and tart lemon, this risotto makes an ordinary dinner seem like a gourmet experience. Go with the ambience and light a few candles. Instant date night! *Serves 8*

1 pound asparagus, trimmed and cut into 1-inch pieces

¼ cup olive oil

1 teaspoon salt

½ teaspoon freshly ground black pepper

6 cups chicken stock, homemade (page 192) or store bought

3 shallots, chopped (about ½ cup)

½ teaspoon red pepper flakes

1¼ cups Arborio rice

2 tablespoons unsalted butter

½ cup grated Asiago cheese (2 ounces)

2 tablespoons grated lemon zest

2 tablespoons lemon juice

1 tablespoon chopped fresh parsley

1 Preheat the oven to 450°F.

2 On a baking sheet, toss the asparagus with 1 tablespoon of the oil. Spread the asparagus in an even layer and season with ½ teaspoon salt and ¼ teaspoon black pepper. Roast until tender, 7 to 10 minutes, depending on the width of the asparagus.

3 In a medium saucepan set over medium-high heat, bring the chicken stock to a simmer. Reduce the heat and keep the stock warm over low heat.

4 In a large saucepan set over medium-high heat, heat the remaining 3 tablespoons of oil. Add the shallots and red pepper flakes and sauté until the shallots begin to soften, 5 to 7 minutes.

5 Add the rice to the saucepan, and cook, stirring, for 4 minutes, until the rice is coated in oil and starts to toast. Add the warm stock, a little at a time and stirring often, until all the liquid has been absorbed into the rice, making it tender but not mushy, about 18 minutes.

6 Stir in the butter, cheese, lemon zest, lemon juice, and parsley. Remove the pan from the heat and fold in the asparagus. Season with remaining salt and black pepper.

This dish can be made VEGETARIAN by substituting vegetable stock (page 194) for the chicken stock.

NENE'S SPANISH RICE

Sandy loves her brother-in-law, but she loves his mother, Irene, the best! Everyone calls her Nene, and she makes the best Spanish rice in the Rio Grande Valley. There's a lot **GLUTEN-FREE** of Spanish rice in the valley, but this recipe puts the others to shame. And it's simple! Fresh bell peppers, onions, and tomato sauce make this dish lively. Serve it with our Chicken Enchiladas (page 68) and Red, Red Wine Sangria (page 23), and any day can be Cinco de Mayo! *Serves 8*

3 cups chicken stock, homemade (page 192) or store bought

3 tablespoons vegetable oil

1½ cups long-grain white rice

½ red bell pepper, chopped

½ large onion, chopped

3 garlic cloves, chopped

1 teaspoon ground cumin

1 teaspoon salt

½ teaspoon freshly ground black pepper

½ cup tomato sauce

1 In a medium saucepan set over medium-high heat, heat the chicken stock. Keep it warm over low heat.

2 In a large sauté pan set over medium heat, heat the oil. Add the rice and cook for about 5 minutes, stirring occasionally, until it browns. Add the red bell pepper, onion, and garlic, and cook for 2 minutes. Add the cumin, salt, and black pepper, and stir well.

3 Add 2½ cups of the warm chicken stock and the tomato sauce to the rice mixture. Reduce the heat to low, cover the pan, and simmer for 15 minutes, or until the liquid has completely absorbed. If the rice is too dry, add more chicken stock, ¼ cup at a time.

This dish can be made **VEGETARIAN** by substituting vegetable stock (page 194) for the chicken stock.

ROYAL
Ratatouille

Ratatouille is the French term for "all the healthy and delicious veggies you need in one scrumptious serving." Well, not really, but that's how we think of it. A hearty dish  of stewed vegetables, it's a perfect accompaniment to heavier meats like beef and lamb, but it's also great as a side dish to eggs. We love it alongside our "Sitch" Chicken Parmesan (see page 64). It's the kind of dish whose leftovers taste even better the next day when the flavors have had more of a chance to develop. Ratatouille sounds and tastes complicated, but it really comes down to chopping, seasoning, and layering. Easy, and the results are *magnifique!* *Serves 8*

½ cup olive oil

1 medium eggplant, cut into ¼-inch-thick slices

1 large yellow onion, cut into ¼-inch-thick slices

1 green bell pepper, cut into rings

4 Roma tomatoes, sliced into ¼-inch-thick slices

2 garlic cloves, thinly sliced

2 jalapeño peppers, seeded and finely chopped

Salt and freshly ground black pepper

½ teaspoon sugar

1 teaspoon dried basil

3 small zucchini, cut into ¼-inch-thick slices

½ cup chopped fresh parsley

3 yellow squash, cut into ¼-inch-thick slices

1 teaspoon dried oregano

1 Preheat the oven to 350°F.

2 Put 2 tablespoons of the oil in the bottom of a 9 x 13-inch casserole dish. Make one layer of each of the ingredients, in the following order: all of the eggplant and a third of the onions, bell peppers, tomatoes, garlic, and jalapeño peppers. Sprinkle with salt, pepper, and a pinch of the sugar. Drizzle 2 tablespoons of oil over the layer and sprinkle with the basil.

3 Make a second layer of each of the ingredients, in the following order: all of the zucchini and a third of the onions, bell peppers, tomatoes, garlic, and jalapeños. Sprinkle with salt, pepper, and another pinch of the sugar. Drizzle 2 tablespoons of oil over the layer and sprinkle with parsley.

4 Make a final layer of each of the ingredients, in the following order: all of the yellow squash and the remaining onions, bell peppers, tomatoes, garlic, and jalapeño peppers. Sprinkle with salt, pepper, and the remaining sugar. Drizzle the remaining 2 tablespoons of oil over the top and sprinkle with the oregano.

5 Cover and bake until the vegetables are tender, about 1 hour. Serve hot.

This recipe can be made DIABETIC-FRIENDLY by substituting a pinch of stevia for the sugar. Note that you only need a pinch, as stevia is about 300 times sweeter than sugar.

Ratatouille does involve a lot of chopping, but if you want to cut the prep work in half, simply remember your kitchen appliances! Most kitchen tools are created to make tasks easier. So why are they sitting there taking up space and collecting dust? Remember, folks, you registered for them for a reason, so let's put them to work! One of the Queens' most trusted appliances is the food processor. Food processers can do all of your slicing, dicing, shredding, and pureeing in seconds, and with all the cooking you'll be doing from this book (subtle hint), it's not only important to save time in the kitchen, it's also important to save your wrists!

WILD RICE

Chock-full of hearty mushrooms and tasty vegetables, this recipe turns boring rice into something wild! A flavorful and savory dish with the nutty accent of toasted almonds, it's truly something to roar about. We think this dish perfectly complements our Chicken with 40 Cloves of Garlic (page 43)! *Serves 8*

9 tablespoons unsalted butter

1 cup wild rice

2 (10½-ounce) cans beef consommé

1 pound button mushrooms, sliced

½ medium red bell pepper, chopped

1 bunch green onions, green parts only, sliced

¼ cup chopped fresh parsley

1 teaspoon salt

½ teaspoon freshly ground black pepper

½ cup slivered almonds, toasted

1 Preheat the oven to 350°F. Grease a 9 x 13-inch casserole dish with 1 tablespoon of the butter.

2 Rinse the rice well under running water and drain. In a large saucepan set over medium heat, combine the rice with 2 cups of the consommé. Bring the mixture to a boil. Reduce the heat to low, cover the pan, and simmer until the liquid is absorbed, about 30 minutes.

3 In a large skillet set over medium-high heat, melt 4 tablespoons of butter. Add the mushrooms, bell pepper, and green onions and cook for 5 minutes, until tender. Add the parsley, salt, pepper, and almonds and stir well. Pour the vegetable mixture into the pan of cooked rice and stir well. Pour the mixture into the prepared casserole dish. Refrigerate, covered, for at least 2 hours and up to 2 days.

4 Take the dish out of the refrigerator, dot with the remaining 4 tablespoons of butter, and add the remaining consommé. Cover the dish with foil and bake for 30 to 40 minutes, or until the consommé has been absorbed. Serve hot. If not serving immediately, let the rice cool completely and store in an airtight container in the refrigerator for up to 1 week.

SIMPLE HERB-ROASTED
Vegetables

This recipe reminds Crystal of her college days in Boston. During the long, cold winter months (which seemed to last until early May), she loved nothing more than loading up her plate with some warm and filling roasted vegetables. Pair this with our BBQ Pork Ribs (page 37) or our Awesome Aussie Meat Pies (page 70) and a big ol' glass of ale, and you'll be able to brave the cold another day. *Serves 8*

GLUTEN-FREE

VEGETARIAN!

Cooking spray

1 bunch fresh parsley, chopped

1 bunch fresh basil, chopped

3 garlic cloves, minced

1/2 teaspoon red pepper flakes

1 cup vegetable oil

2 pounds red potatoes, quartered

1 red bell pepper, chopped

1 zucchini, chopped

1 pound carrots, peeled and chopped

1 teaspoon salt

1/2 teaspoon freshly ground black pepper

1 Preheat the oven to 425°F. Spray an 8 x 13-inch rimmed baking sheet (half sheet pan) with cooking spray.

2 In a blender, pulse the parsley, basil, garlic, red pepper flakes, and oil until smooth. You're looking for the consistency of Italian vinaigrette, so add more oil if the mixture needs thinning.

3 In a large bowl, combine the potatoes, bell pepper, zucchini, and carrots. Add the blended herb sauce, salt, and black pepper. Toss well to coat. Spread the vegetables in a single layer on the prepared baking sheet.

4 Roast for about 40 minutes, or until the vegetables are tender and a bit browned. Serve right away.

CURRIED RICE
Veggie Bake

The Queens have long been believers in the healing power of curry, but lately they've been hearing a lot of good things about the health benefits of turmeric. This bright yellow-orange spice has been used as a powerful anti-inflammatory  in traditional Chinese and Indian medicine for centuries. Recently, it has proven to be beneficial in the treatment of many health conditions, including Alzheimer's disease and arthritis. We like it because it adds a warm, peppery flavor and a beautiful color to this dish. *Serves 6 to 8*

Cooking spray

1 tablespoon vegetable oil

1 onion, chopped

1 garlic clove, crushed

2 tablespoons curry powder

3 sweet potatoes, peeled and diced

1 red bell pepper, chopped

1 (15-ounce) can diced tomatoes

1 (8-ounce) bag fresh spinach

2 cups cooked rice (see page 199)

1 large egg, beaten

2 cups grated Gruyère cheese (8 ounces)

2 cups seasoned bread crumbs, homemade (see page 188) or store bought

¼ cup chopped fresh cilantro

¼ teaspoon ground turmeric

1 Preheat the oven to 400°F. Spray a 9 x 13-inch casserole dish with cooking spray.

2 In a medium sauté pan set over medium-high heat, heat the oil. Add the onion and garlic and cook, stirring, until slightly browned, about 5 minutes. Add the curry powder and cook for 2 more minutes. If the onion starts to dry out, add a couple of tablespoons of water to the pan. Add the sweet potatoes, bell pepper, and tomatoes, cover, and simmer for 10 minutes, until the veggies start to soften. Remove the lid and stir in the spinach. Cook for 5 more minutes, or until the sauce has reduced and thickened.

3 Put the rice in a bowl and add the egg and 1 cup of the cheese. Stir well and scoop out into the prepared casserole dish. Press the rice down into the dish, then pour the vegetable mixture on top.

4 In a medium bowl, combine the remaining 1 cup of cheese and the bread crumbs, cilantro, and turmeric. Sprinkle the mixture over the top of the vegetables. Bake for 20 minutes, or until the top is brown and crispy.

FREEZES WELL! For best results, prepare the casserole through step 3. Wrap in foil and freeze for up to 2 months. Thaw the casserole overnight in the refrigerator. The next day, prepare the bread crumb topping (step 4) and bake as stated in the recipe. Note that casseroles that have not been completely thawed may take 15 to 30 minutes longer, so be sure to check for bubbling edges and a hot center.

This dish can be made **GLUTEN-FREE** by using gluten-free bread crumbs, either store bought (see page 15 for recommendations of our favorite brands) or homemade (see page 188 for our recipe).

DILL BREAD

The recipe calls for a casserole dish, but we love using our cast-iron skillet. It gives the bread a more rustic feel—so homey and comforting. The incorporation of dill seed gives each wedge a delightfully herbal pop, making it a nice complement to most any meal. We particularly love it with our Shepherdless Pie (page 93) and Chicken Casserole: A Cook Family Favorite (page 106). *Serves 8*

VEGETARIAN!

Cooking spray

¼ cup (½ stick) unsalted butter

2 cups small-curd cottage cheese

½ cup whole milk

2 (¼-ounce) packages dry yeast

4 to 4½ cups all-purpose flour

¼ cup sugar

1 small onion, finely chopped

2 large eggs

4 teaspoons dill seed

2 teaspoons salt

½ teaspoon baking soda

1 Spray a 9 x 13-inch casserole dish with cooking spray.

2 In a medium saucepan set over medium heat, melt the butter. Remove the pan from the heat and stir in the cottage cheese and milk. Sprinkle the yeast over the mixture and gently stir to dissolve. Let sit for 10 minutes.

3 In a large bowl, mix together the flour, sugar, onion, eggs, dill seed, salt, and baking soda. Add the yeast mixture to the flour mixture and mix just until incorporated. Don't overwork. Cover the bowl with a damp towel and let the dough rise for 1 hour.

4 Punch down the dough and transfer it to the prepared casserole dish. Cover and let rise for 40 minutes. Preheat the oven to 350°F.

5 Uncover the dish and bake the bread for 30 to 40 minutes, or until golden brown.

This dish can be made GLUTEN-FREE by replacing the flour with a gluten-free all-purpose mix, either store bought (see page 15 for recommendations of our favorite brands) or homemade (see page 186 for our recipe).

POTATOES TWO TIMES
with a Kick Casserole

Crystal's nieces, Alexis and Cassie, are like most sisters close in age: they are the best of friends and mortal enemies at the same time. Even though they love each other dearly, neither of them is so gracious as to offer the last twice-baked potato to the other. Instead, they wage an all-out war over who eats the last one. In hopes of creating some world peace, we have transformed twice-baked potatoes into a large, filling casserole. This way, there should be plenty for all!

GLUTEN-FREE

Serves 10

10 large russet potatoes

4 cups shredded Colby Jack cheese (16 ounces)

1 pound bacon, cooked and crumbled

1 bunch green onions, green parts only, chopped

½ cup pickled jalapeños, chopped

3 large eggs, lightly beaten

1½ cups sour cream

½ cup (1 stick) plus 1 tablespoon unsalted butter, at room temperature

2 teaspoons salt

1 teaspoon freshly ground black pepper

10 dashes Tabasco sauce (or more if you like)

Cooking spray

1 Preheat the oven to 400°F.

2 Poke the potatoes with a fork all over. Bake the potatoes on a rimmed baking sheet for about 1 hour, or until tender. Remove from the oven and let cool.

3 Once the potatoes are cool, scrape off all of the skins and discard. Put the inside of the potatoes in a large bowl and mash until semi-smooth. Add 2½ cups of the cheese, the bacon, green onions, jalapeños, eggs, sour cream, butter, salt, pepper, and Tabasco sauce. Mix well.

4 Reduce the oven temperature to 375°F. Spray a 9 x 13-inch casserole dish with cooking spray.

5 Pour the potato mixture into the prepared casserole dish and top with the remaining 1½ cups cheese. Bake for 35 to 40 minutes, or until the mixture is heated through and bubbling around the edges.

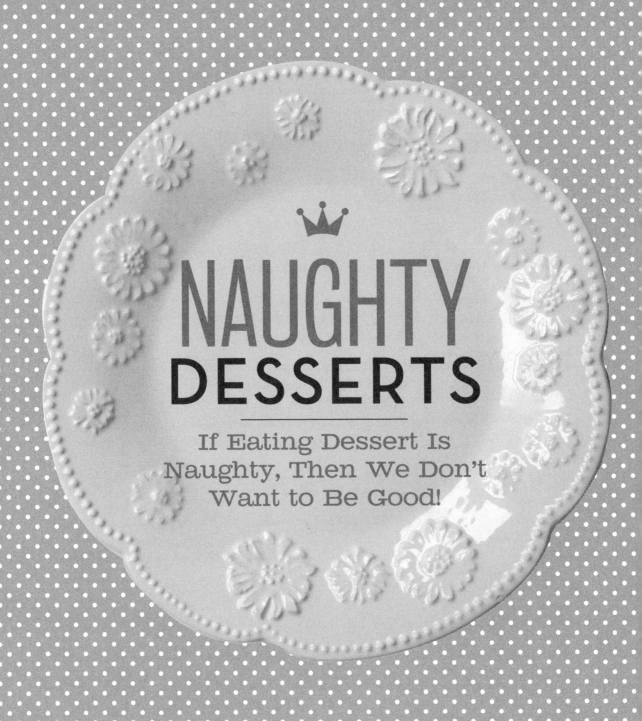

NAUGHTY
DESSERTS

If Eating Dessert Is
Naughty, Then We Don't
Want to Be Good!

We love casseroles and think they are perfection, but let's face it—a meal isn't truly perfect until you have dessert! So let's get a little naughty in the kitchen, shall we? We're whipping up sexy dishes such as Key West Clafouti (page 164), decadent Buttermilk Cake with Malted Chocolate Frosting (page 175), comforting Apple Crunch Coffee Cake (page 171), tangy Frozen Lemon Dessert (page 178), and oh so much more. Some of our recipes are over the top, like our S'more Pie (page 176) and Pecan Squares (page 168), while others just have a hint of sweetness, like Granny Haley's Angel Food Cake with Vanilla Strawberry Sauce (page 172). Now, enough with the teasing, let's start baking love!

- KEY WEST CLAFOUTI

- BROWNIES

- PECAN SQUARES

- HOT FUDGE SUNDAE CAKE

- PRETZEL NUT NILLA CAKE

- APPLE CRUNCH COFFEE CAKE

- GRANNY HALEY'S ANGEL FOOD CAKE WITH VANILLA STRAWBERRY SAUCE

- GRANNY PANSY'S BAKED APPLES

- BUTTERMILK CAKE WITH MALTED CHOCOLATE FROSTING

- S'MORE PIE

- FROZEN LEMON DESSERT

- EASY MAPLE SOPAPILLA CASSEROLE

- AUSTIN CHEWIES

KEY WEST
Clafouti

Clafouti Tootie, Fresh and Fruity! Sorry, we couldn't help ourselves. Traditionally made with cherries, a clafouti is a fluffy, fruit-filled French dessert. The batter is similar to that of pancakes (which makes this dish great for brunch, too), and it is dusted with a layer of powdered sugar for serving. Umm . . . yum! In our version, we have veered away from the traditional tart cherries, opting for tropical fruits like mango, lime, and coconut. The fruit is arranged in the bottom of a baking dish and then covered with a batter spiked with some Malibu rum. This dish is best served straight from the oven, because even though it puffs up nicely, it can deflate rather quickly. *Serves 8*

2 tablespoons unsalted butter, melted, plus more for the pan

2 ripe mangoes, peeled and diced

1/2 cup coconut rum, such as Malibu

1 cup sweetened coconut flakes

5 large eggs, lightly beaten

1¼ cups heavy cream

1¼ cups whole milk

1 teaspoon grated lime zest

1 cup granulated sugar

2/3 cup all-purpose flour, sifted

Confectioners' sugar, for dusting

1 Preheat the oven to 325°F. Butter a 9 x 13-inch casserole dish.

2 Put the mangoes and the rum in a large bowl and let sit for 1 hour to allow the mangoes to absorb the liquid.

3 Put the coconut in a single layer on a baking sheet. Toast for 12 to 15 minutes, until golden brown. Transfer to a large plate and let cool.

4 Increase the oven temperature to 350°F.

5 In a large bowl, whisk together the eggs, melted butter, cream, milk, and lime zest.

6 In a separate large bowl, whisk together the granulated sugar and flour, and stir in the coconut. Stir the coconut mixture into the egg mixture.

7 Spread the mango-rum mixture in the bottom of the prepared casserole dish. Top with the batter.

8 Bake for 35 minutes, or until cooked through and golden. Let cool for 5 minutes, sprinkle with the confectioners' sugar, and serve. Store in an airtight container in the refrigerator for up to a week.

This dish can be made GLUTEN-FREE by replacing the flour with a gluten-free all-purpose mix, either store bought (see page 15 for recommendations of our favorite brands) or homemade (see page 186 for our recipe). Also, be sure to look over the ingredients in the rum for any barley, wheat, or rye.

BROWNIES

Early in life, you have to make certain decisions. For example, are you a cookie person or a brownie person? Both of the Queens' men—Tim and Michael—are cookie monsters, but we Queens love ourselves a good brownie! While the recipe calls for serving them with our homemade caramel sauce—which makes them oh-so-decadent—these brownies can stand perfectly on their own. If you're keen on dressing them up, we have included a recipe for our favorite blackberry coulis, too. *Makes 20 brownies*

1 tablespoon unsalted butter, softened, for buttering the dish

2 cups bittersweet chocolate chips (you can use milk chocolate, if you prefer)

1⅓ cups vegetable oil

2 teaspoons vanilla extract

2 cups sugar

4 large eggs

2 cups all-purpose flour

1½ teaspoons salt

1 teaspoon baking powder

1½ cups chopped pecans

Caramel Sauce, optional (page 202), or Blackberry Coulis, optional (opposite)

1 Preheat the oven to 325°F. Butter a 9 x 13-inch casserole dish.

2 Put a glass bowl over a small saucepan of simmering water. Put the chocolate, oil, and vanilla in the bowl and let them heat gently, stirring constantly until the chocolate melts completely. Set aside until cool to the touch, about 20 minutes.

3 In a large bowl, whisk together the sugar and eggs until the mixture is a light yellow color, about 5 minutes. While whisking, slowly pour in the chocolate mixture and whisk until well combined.

4 In a separate bowl, sift together the flour, salt, and baking powder. Add the dry ingredients to the chocolate mixture and stir well. Stir in the nuts.

5 Spread the batter into the prepared casserole dish. Bake for 35 minutes, or until a toothpick inserted into the center comes out clean. Let cool for 5 minutes before cutting. Serve as is or with Caramel Sauce or Blackberry Coulis. Store in an airtight container in the refrigerator for up to 1 week.

This dish can be made GLUTEN-FREE by replacing the flour with a gluten-free all-purpose mix, either store bought (see page 15 for recommendations of our favorite brands) or homemade (see page 186 for our recipe). Also, be sure to use a gluten-free baking powder.

Blackberry Coulis

MAKES 3 CUPS

Because what goes better with chocolate than red wine!

¾ cup fruity red wine
6 tablespoons sugar
1 pint blackberries (about 3 cups)

In a heavy-bottomed saucepan set over high heat, combine the wine and sugar and bring to a boil. Boil for 2 minutes, until the sugar dissolves. Turn the heat down to medium and simmer for 10 minutes more, to allow the sauce to reduce a bit. Add the berries and bring the mixture back up to a simmer, then cook (don't boil) for 3 minutes. Take the pan off the heat and let the berries cool in the wine syrup.

PECAN SQUARES

A rite of passage for all Southern girls is perfecting the art of the pecan pie. Since Crystal is far from perfect, she found an easier way to showcase her sweet skills. These squares will definitely earn you your Southern-girl kitchen credibility. They are ooey, gooey, and delicious—and a cinch to prepare! *Serves 8*

1½ cups (3 sticks) unsalted butter, cold, divided, plus more for pan

2 cups all-purpose flour

⅔ cup confectioners' sugar

½ cup firmly packed light brown sugar

½ cup honey

3 tablespoons heavy cream

3½ cups coarsely chopped pecans

1 Preheat the oven to 350°F. Lightly butter a 9 x 13-inch casserole dish.

2 In a medium bowl, sift together the flour and confectioners' sugar. Using a pastry blender or two forks, cut ¾ cup of the butter into the flour mixture until it resembles a coarse meal. Pat the mixture on the bottom and 1½ inches up the sides of the prepared casserole dish. Bake for 20 minutes, or until golden brown. Remove the dish from the oven and let cool.

3 In a saucepan set over medium-high heat, melt the remaining ¾ cup of butter. Add the brown sugar, honey, and cream, and bring the mixture to a boil. Stir in the pecans and pour the hot filling into the prepared crust. Bake for 25 to 30 minutes, or until golden and bubbly. Let cool for 5 minutes before cutting into 2-inch squares. Store in an airtight container in the refrigerator for up to 1 week.

This dish can be made GLUTEN-FREE by replacing the flour with a gluten-free all-purpose mix, either store bought (see page 15 for recommendations of our favorite brands) or homemade (see page 186 for our recipe).

HOT FUDGE
Sundae Cake

It's a question we've all asked ourselves at one time or another: do I treat myself to a sundae, or am I more in the mood for a piece of cake? But why decide between two limiting options when you can have the best of both worlds? Sunday may be fun day, but this decadent cake served with vanilla ice cream is a treat for any day of the week. *Serves 8*

1 cup all-purpose flour

3/4 cup granulated sugar

1/4 cup plus 2 tablespoons Dutch-processed cocoa powder

2 teaspoons baking powder

1/4 teaspoon salt

1/2 cup whole milk

2 tablespoons vegetable oil

1 teaspoon vanilla extract

1 cup chopped pecans

1 cup packed dark brown sugar

1 3/4 cups hot water

Vanilla ice cream

1 Preheat the oven to 350°F.

2 In an ungreased 9 x 13-inch casserole dish, stir together the flour, granulated sugar, 2 tablespoons of the cocoa powder, the baking powder, and salt.

3 In a medium bowl, combine the milk, oil, and vanilla. Pour the liquid mixture into the casserole dish and stir well with a fork. Stir in the pecans and spread the mixture, pressing evenly into the casserole dish. Sprinkle the top with the brown sugar and the remaining 1/4 cup of cocoa powder. Pour the hot water evenly over the batter.

4 Bake for 40 minutes, or until a toothpick inserted into the center of the cake comes out clean. Remove the dish from the oven and let cool for 15 minutes. Serve with a scoop of vanilla ice cream.

5 Store the cake in an airtight container in the refrigerator for up to a week.

This dish can be made GLUTEN-FREE by replacing the flour with a gluten-free all-purpose mix, either store bought (see page 15 for recommendations of our favorite brands) or homemade (see page 186 for our recipe). Also, be sure to use a gluten-free baking powder.

PRETZEL NUT
Nilla Cake

In the South, we call vanilla wafers *'nilla* wafers. Just like we call pudding *puddin'*. Hmm . . . come to think of it, bet the person who invented Nilla wafers was from the South, as we Southerners tend to lose the extra parts of words so we can get right to the good stuff. This cake is all kinds of good stuff—vanilla wafers, peanuts, and pretzels— in one delicious dessert. Try it and you just may start droppin' letters and syllables like a Southerner. Who needs them, anyhow, when your mouth is full of cake? *Serves 8*

Cooking spray

1 cup granulated sugar

1 cup packed dark brown sugar

¾ cup (1½ sticks) unsalted butter, softened

6 large eggs

½ cup whole milk

1 teaspoon vanilla extract

20 vanilla wafers, crushed

1 cup unsalted peanuts, chopped

1 cup thin pretzel rods, coarsely chopped

1 Preheat the oven to 350°F. Spray a 9 x 13-inch casserole dish with cooking spray.

2 In a large bowl, cream together the granulated sugar, brown sugar, and butter. Add the eggs, milk, vanilla, vanilla wafers, peanuts, and pretzels. Mix thoroughly. Pour the mixture into the prepared casserole dish.

3 Bake for 1 hour, or until a toothpick inserted into the center comes out clean. Let cool for 5 minutes before serving.

4 Store the cake in an airtight container in the refrigerator for up to 1 week.

APPLE CRUNCH
Coffee Cake

Cake for breakfast? Sure! If it's wrong, do you really want to be right? We didn't think so. Full of apples and nuts, this versatile cake can be breakfast, dessert, or an afternoon snack. It's all you need to make anytime special. *Serves 16*

½ tablespoon butter, for buttering the dish

2 cups all-purpose flour, plus more for dusting

2 cups Golden Delicious apples, peeled, cored, and chopped

2 cups sugar

1 cup vegetable oil

2 large eggs

2 teaspoons ground cinnamon

2 teaspoons baking powder

½ teaspoon salt

1 cup chopped walnuts

1 Preheat the oven to 350°F. Butter and flour a 9 x 13-inch casserole dish.

2 In a large bowl, combine the apples, flour, sugar, oil, eggs, cinnamon, baking powder, salt, and nuts and stir well. The batter will be thick.

3 Spread the batter in the prepared casserole dish. Bake for 55 minutes, or until a toothpick inserted in the center of the cake comes out clean. Let cool for 5 minutes before serving.

4 Store in an airtight container in the refrigerator for up to 1 week.

This dish can be made GLUTEN-FREE by replacing the flour with a gluten-free all-purpose mix, either store bought (see page 15 for recommendations of our favorite brands) or homemade (see page 186 for our recipe). Also, be sure to use a gluten-free baking powder.

GRANNY HALEY'S ANGEL FOOD CAKE
with Vanilla Strawberry Sauce

Sandy's granny Haley kept a glass Coke bottle in her cabinet for the times she made angel cake. When the cake would come out of the oven, she would flip it over and let it hang on the neck of the Coke bottle to cool. She did this all the time, but the first time Sandy and her sister Kellye saw it, they must have looked very confused, which made Granny Haley giggle like no one's business. Granny Haley's giggle was legendary: her entire body would shimmy and shake, and she would get all flustered, turning fifty different shades of pink and red. Man, she was darling. *Serves 8*

1 cup cake flour

1¾ cups sugar

12 egg whites, at room temperature

1½ teaspoons cream of tartar

¼ teaspoon salt

2 teaspoons vanilla extract

1 pint strawberries, washed, hulled, and sliced

1 tablespoon cornstarch

1 tablespoon unsalted butter

8 mint leaves for garnish

1 Preheat the oven to 375°F.

2 Sift together the flour and ¾ cup of the sugar.

3 In a large bowl, beat the egg whites with the cream of tartar, salt, and 1½ teaspoons of the vanilla until stiff enough to hold soft peaks, but still moist and glossy, about 5 minutes. While beating, add ¾ cup of the sugar, 2 teaspoons at a time. Continue to beat until the meringue holds stiff peaks.

4 Sift about a quarter of the flour mixture over the meringue, and using a rubber spatula, gently fold in the flour. Fold in the remaining flour, a quarter at a time.

5 Pour the batter into an ungreased Bundt pan. Bake for 35 to 40 minutes, until a toothpick inserted in the center comes out clean.

6 Meanwhile, put the strawberries in a bowl and sprinkle them with the remaining ¼ cup of sugar. Let them stand for 15 minutes. Stir occasionally. Drain the berries, reserving the juice. Add enough water to the juice to make 1 cup of liquid. In a medium saucepan set over medium heat, combine the cornstarch and the juice and cook, stirring constantly, until the mixture thickens, about 7 minutes. Stir in the butter, and then fold in the berries and the remaining ½ teaspoon of vanilla.

7 Let the cake cool completely in the pan. Then invert the pan onto a cutting board to release the cake, and slice the cake into 8 wedges. Garnish with the mint leaves and extra strawberries, if desired. Serve with the strawberry sauce.

This dish can be made GLUTEN-FREE by eliminating the regular cake flour and substituting a gluten-free cake flour mix. We recommend Pamela's brand. Also, be sure to use a gluten-free cornstarch.

GRANNY PANSY'S
Baked Apples

Even in the Rio Grande Valley of Texas, the temperatures start cooling down in late autumn. This dish always reminds Sandy of spending chilly fall afternoons in her granny  Pansy's kitchen. Granny Pansy knew that these were the perfect midday treat when the air started getting crisp and apples were in season. Not too heavy and not involved, just the thing when you're hankering for a little something sweet—just like Granny Pansy! *Serves 6*

½ cup granulated sugar

6 Golden Delicious apples

⅓ cup packed light brown sugar

3 tablespoons unsalted butter, softened

1 teaspoon ground cinnamon

Vanilla ice cream

1 Preheat the oven to 375°F.

2 In a saucepan set over medium heat, combine the granulated sugar with 1 cup of water. Cook until the sugar dissolves, about 4 minutes. Pour the syrup into the bottom of a 9 x 13-inch casserole dish.

3 Core the apples, but don't go all the way through to the bottom. (This will help keep the sugar filling in the apple.) In a medium bowl, mix the brown sugar, butter, and cinnamon thoroughly. Divide the mixture equally among the 6 apples. Put the filled apples in the casserole dish.

4 Bake for 45 minutes to 1 hour, or until a knife can be easily inserted into the apples. Let cool for 5 minutes. Serve with vanilla ice cream.

BUTTERMILK CAKE
with Malted Chocolate Frosting

Crystal's friend Martha is known for stealing all of the malt balls out of her children's Halloween treat bags. Though she tries not to do it, she finds them so deliciously sweet and addictive, she simply can't help herself. She spends the day after Halloween with a toothache, a remorseful conscience, and three angry boys. Thanks to this cake, she no longer has to resort to petty theft to get her malty fix. Don't worry; this rich cake won't cause a toothache . . . and you don't have to wait until Halloween to try it! *Serves 12*

1½ cups (3 sticks) unsalted butter, softened, plus more for the dish

4 cups cake flour

1 teaspoon baking soda

½ teaspoon baking powder

1 teaspoon salt

3 cups granulated sugar

3 teaspoons vanilla extract

2 cups buttermilk

6 large egg whites

4 teaspoons light corn syrup

¼ cup unsweetened cocoa powder

½ cup malted milk powder

1½ cups confectioners' sugar

3 to 4 tablespoons heavy cream

1 Preheat the oven to 350°F. Butter a 9 x13-inch casserole dish.

2 Sift together the flour, baking soda, baking powder, and ½ teaspoon of the salt.

3 In the bowl of an electric mixer fitted with the whisk attachment, cream 1 cup of the butter with the granulated sugar until light and fluffy, about 3 minutes. Beat in 1½ teaspoons of the vanilla. Add the flour mixture to the creamed butter and sugar alternately with the buttermilk, beating well after each addition. Add the egg whites and beat at medium speed for about 1 minute. Pour the batter into the prepared dish. Bake for 20 minutes. Reduce the heat to 325°F and bake for 25 more minutes. Let the cake cool in the dish.

4 Meanwhile, in small bowl, whisk the remaining ½ cup of butter, the corn syrup, and the remaining 1½ teaspoons of vanilla. Add the cocoa powder, the remaining ½ teaspoon of salt, and the malted milk powder, and whisk until well blended. Add the confectioners' sugar and 3 tablespoons of the heavy cream. If the frosting is too thick, add more cream until you reach a good spreading consistency. Frost the top of the cake.

S'MORE PIE

In Texas, the camping months are rather limited for those of us who do not enjoy sleeping in a steam room. But everyone knows that the best part of a camping trip is the dessert! Now you can avoid all the bug spray and sleeping on the ground and get your chocolate-marshmallow-graham fix in a pie you make at home. May I get s'more, please? *Serves 10*

Cooking spray

8 graham crackers

1/3 cup packed dark brown sugar

2 1/2 tablespoons unsalted butter, melted

3/4 teaspoon salt

14 ounces semisweet chocolate, finely chopped

2 cups heavy cream

2 large eggs, at room temperature

1 (10-ounce) bag mini marshmallows

1 Preheat the oven to 350°F. Spray a 9 x 13-inch casserole dish with cooking spray.

2 In a food processor, pulse the graham crackers until finely ground. Add the brown sugar, butter, and 1/2 teaspoon of the salt, and process until well combined. Press the crumb mixture into the bottom and up the sides of the prepared casserole dish. Bake for 10 minutes, then let cool completely.

3 Put the chocolate in a large, heatproof bowl and set aside. In a large, heavy saucepan set over medium-high heat, bring the cream just to a boil, about 5 minutes. Pour the hot cream over the chocolate. Let it stand for 1 minute, then gently whisk until the chocolate is melted and the mixture is smooth. Gently whisk in the eggs and the remaining 1/4 teaspoon of salt until combined. Pour the filling into the graham cracker crust (it will fill the crust about halfway).

4 Bake for about 25 minutes, or just until the center becomes slightly firm. Let cool for 10 minutes.

5 Preheat the oven to Broil.

6 Cover the entire top of the casserole with the marshmallows. Don't let any brown peek through! Put the marshmallow-covered casserole back in the oven 3 to 4 inches from the heat and broil, rotating casserole as necessary, until the marshmallows are golden brown, about 3 minutes. Watch this step very closely, as they can go from browned to burnt in a second. Allow to cool for 10 minutes before serving.

7 Store in an airtight container in the refrigerator for up to 1 week.

This dish can be made GLUTEN-FREE by replacing the regular graham crackers with a gluten-free brand. We recommend Kinnikinnick S'moreables Graham Style Crackers.

FROZEN LEMON
Dessert

A little slice of sunshine on a plate! Cool and tart, this refreshingly simple dessert packs a ton of lemon flavor that will instantly bring a smile to your face. Take advantage of your sunny disposition by doubling the batch so that you will have an extra on hand to share with surprise guests. That is, unless you are not a fan of the unexpected pop-in. In that case, draw the shades and keep that extra dessert to yourself. We won't tell!

Serves 10

Unsalted butter, softened, for the dish

60 vanilla wafers, crushed (about 3 cups)

1/2 cup sugar

3 large eggs, separated

3 tablespoons fresh lemon juice (from 2 lemons)

1/4 teaspoon salt

1 cup heavy cream

1 Butter a 9 x 13-inch casserole dish. Sprinkle 1½ cups of the crushed vanilla wafers on the bottom of the dish; set aside.

2 In a medium heatproof bowl, combine the sugar, egg yolks, lemon juice, and salt, and whisk until the mixture is light yellow in color, about 6 minutes.

3 Set a medium saucepan over medium heat and pour in ½ inch of water. Bring the water to a simmer. Put the bowl of the sugar–egg yolk mixture over the simmering water and whisk constantly until the sauce is thick enough to coat the back of a metal spoon. Remove the bowl from the pan and let the mixture cool completely.

4 In a separate bowl, beat the egg whites until they hold stiff peaks. Fold them into the cooled sugar–egg yolk mixture.

5 In another separate bowl, whip the heavy cream until it holds stiff peaks. Fold it into the cooled sugar-egg mixture. Pour the mixture into the prepared dish and sprinkle the top with the remaining 1½ cups of crushed vanilla wafers. Freeze until solid, for at least 2 hours.

ⓢ When ready to serve, let it sit at room temperature for 10 minutes before cutting. Store the leftovers in the refrigerator for 2 days.

FREEZES WELL! This dessert will keep in the freezer for 2 months.

This dish can be made GLUTEN-FREE by eliminating the vanilla wafer crumbs and substituting gluten-free cookies. See page 15 for recommendations of our favorite gluten-free brands.

EASY MAPLE SOPAPILLA
Casserole

Sopapillas are a damn-tasty deep-fried pastry drizzled in honey or syrup, or sprinkled with powdered sugar or cinnamon. They are a popular dessert in South America and New Mexico, as well as in many of Austin's wonderful Tex-Mex restaurants. Our version is not deep fried and combines the sweet pastry goodness of the sopapilla with the creamy decadence of cheesecake. ¡Muy delicioso! *Serves 16*

Cooking spray

2 sheets frozen puff pastry, thawed

Flour for work surface

¼ cup honey

3 (8-ounce) packages cream cheese, softened

1½ cups packed brown sugar

1 teaspoon maple extract

1 cup (2 sticks) unsalted butter, melted

¼ cup granulated sugar

1 teaspoon ground cinnamon

1 Preheat the oven to 350°F. Spray a 9 x 13-inch casserole dish with cooking spray.

2 Take 1 sheet of the puff pastry and lay it out on a floured work surface. Roll it out to fit in the prepared casserole dish. Lay the pastry in the bottom of the prepared casserole dish. Using a fork, poke holes in the pastry, and then bake for 10 minutes to partially cook the pastry. Remove the dish from the oven and let cool.

3 In a large bowl, whisk together the honey, cream cheese, brown sugar, and the maple extract. Spread the mixture over the cooled puff pastry.

4 Take the second sheet of puff pastry and lay it out on a floured work surface. Roll it out to fit in the casserole dish. Lay the dough on top of the cream cheese mixture and cut slits into the top so that the pastry won't puff too high when baking. Pour the melted butter over the top.

5 In a small bowl, combine the granulated sugar with the ground cinnamon. Sprinkle the cinnamon-sugar mixture evenly over the top of the casserole.

6 Bake for 30 to 35 minutes. Remove from the oven and let cool for 10 minutes before serving.

Although this makes a great dessert, these sweet puffs are also great with a cup of joe for breakfast. Think of sopapillas as the Tex-Mex alternative to coffee cake or beignets!

AUSTIN
Chewies

A little sweet and nutty, just like Austin. If you can't be here, keeping it weird, at least you can make yourself a batch of these. And if you aren't big on chocolate (we suggest you immediately go see a doctor), this recipe will work equally well with butterscotch or peanut butter chips. Heck, you could even do a combination of all three! Just use 1 cup of each instead of 3 cups of chocolate chips. *Serves 10*

2½ cups sweetened coconut flakes

¾ cup (1½ sticks) unsalted butter, melted

2 cups packed dark brown sugar

2 large eggs, beaten

4 teaspoons vanilla extract

2 cups all-purpose flour

1 teaspoon baking soda

1 teaspoon salt

1 cup pecans, chopped

3 cups chocolate chips

1 (14-ounce) can sweetened condensed milk

6 large egg whites

2¼ cups granulated sugar

1 Preheat the oven to 300°F.

2 Spread the coconut in a thin layer on a baking sheet. Bake for about 20 minutes, stirring every 5 minutes to make sure that the coconut browns evenly. Transfer the coconut to a bowl and let cool.

3 Increase the oven temperature to 350°F. Pour the butter into a 9 x 13-inch casserole dish.

4 In a large bowl, combine the brown sugar, eggs, and 1 teaspoon of the vanilla. In a separate bowl, whisk together the flour, baking soda, and salt. Gradually add the flour mixture to the egg mixture and stir until combined. Stir in the pecans. Spread the mixture into the prepared dish. Bake for 25 to 30 minutes, or until browned. Remove the dish from the oven and let cool. Keep the oven on.

5 In a medium saucepan set over medium heat, combine 2½ cups of the chocolate chips with the sweetened condensed milk and heat until chocolate chips melt. Pour over the cooled caramel pecan mix in the casserole dish.

6 In the bowl of a stand mixer fitted with the whisk attachment, beat the egg whites at medium-high speed until soft peaks form. Add the remaining 3 teaspoons of vanilla and beat just to incorporate. With the mixer running on medium speed, gradually add the granulated sugar and beat until the egg whites are firm and glossy, about 3 minutes. Using a large rubber spatula, fold in the toasted coconut. Spread the mixture over the chocolate layer and sprinkle with the remaining ½ cup of chocolate chips.

7 Put the dessert in the oven for 15 minutes to melt the chocolate and heat through. Serve warm.

This dish can be made GLUTEN-FREE by replacing the flour with a gluten-free all-purpose mix, either store bought (see page 15 for recommendations of our favorite brands) or homemade (see page 186 for our recipe). Also, check the label of your chocolate chips to make sure they are gluten-free as well.

STARTING
FROM SCRATCH

Fall in Love with Your
Kitchen Again!

The basics.

It is easy to lose sight of them when the kids have to be shuffled from school, to basketball practice, to home—and then there's homework! Truth is, we all use convenience items from time to time. For those occasions when you may want to put in a little more time to make something more affordable, or to elevate the taste of your dishes, these recipes are just the ticket! Or, if dietary restrictions make it necessary for you to closely monitor your ingredients, well, then, this section is for you, too! From spice mixture to gluten-free flour mix and pie crust, our from-scratch chapter provides a multitude of easy options for giving your dish the flavor you crave, without additives or preservatives. Go ahead and let the Queens show you how to get back to the basics!

- CARLY'S FAVORITE GLUTEN-FREE FLOUR MIX
- GLUTEN-FREE PIE CRUST
- SEASONED BREAD CRUMBS
- CREOLE SEASONING
- MEXICAN CORNBREAD
- COOK'S CORNBREAD
- CHICKEN STOCK
- BEEF STOCK
- VEGGIE STOCK

- CREAM OF MUSHROOM SOUP
- CREAM OF CHICKEN SOUP
- MARINARA SAUCE
- VERDE SAUCE
- PERFECT RICE EVERY TIME
- ROASTED CHICKEN
- THAT GERMAN FAMILY SAUERKRAUT
- CARAMEL SAUCE
- SPICY BLOODY MARY

Carly's Favorite
GLUTEN-FREE FLOUR MIX

GLUTEN-FREE

VEGETARIAN!

Owner of Nutritional Wisdom, nutritionist Carly Pollack created a perfect gluten-free flour-mix alternative that's just as versatile as traditional flour, plus it is high in fiber! What's not to love? *Makes 5½ cups*

2 cups brown rice flour

1½ cups potato starch

½ cup tapioca flour

½ cup amaranth flour

1 cup quinoa flour

In a large bowl, combine the brown rice flour, potato starch, tapioca flour, amaranth flour, and quinoa flour. Store in an airtight container for up to 6 months.

GLUTEN-FREE PIE CRUST

Ding! Clever recipe alert for a reliable pie crust you'll make again and again! If you

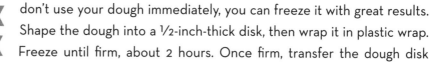

don't use your dough immediately, you can freeze it with great results. Shape the dough into a ½-inch-thick disk, then wrap it in plastic wrap. Freeze until firm, about 2 hours. Once firm, transfer the dough disk to a plastic zip-top freezer bag. The dough will last up to two months in the freezer. *Makes 1 (9-inch) pie crust*

1⅓ cups Carly's Favorite Gluten-Free Flour Mix (opposite), plus more for kneading

1 tablespoon confectioners' sugar (optional)

½ teaspoon salt

½ cup (1 stick) cold unsalted butter, cut into small pieces

1 large egg, lightly beaten

1 Preheat the oven to 375°F.

2 Put the flour mix, sugar (if using), and salt in a food processor and pulse a few times to combine. Add the butter and pulse until the mixture resembles coarse meal. Add the egg and pulse until completely combined.

3 Turn the dough out onto a wooden surface dusted with flour mix. Sprinkle more over the dough and knead gently, working in about 2 more tablespoons of gluten-free flour, until the dough holds together without being sticky but is still very pliable.

4 If not using right away, form a ball with the dough and wrap tightly with plastic wrap. Refrigerate for up to 5 days.

Seasoned
BREAD CRUMBS

Bread is too good of a thing to let go to waste. How many times does your uneaten bread go to the birds? If for some insane reason you didn't eat an entire baguette for dinner, use the leftovers to make some delicious bread crumbs, which are always handy for adding texture to casseroles. Bread crumbs can go stale quickly, so keep them fresh longer by storing them in the freezer. *Makes about 3 cups*

1 loaf day-old bread

2 tablespoons dried thyme or oregano

2 tablespoons dried basil or parsley

1 teaspoon garlic powder

2 teaspoons salt

1/2 teaspoon freshly ground black pepper

1 Preheat the oven to 300°F.

2 Cut the bread into cubes and pulse in a food processor to make coarse crumbs. Spread the crumbs on a baking sheet (use two baking sheets if necessary) and bake for 10 to 15 minutes, stirring halfway through the baking time, until the crumbs have dried. Let cool completely.

3 Return the bread crumbs to the food processor and add the thyme, basil, garlic powder, salt, and pepper. Pulse until the crumbs are finely processed. Store in an airtight container for up to 3 weeks.

This recipe can be made GLUTEN-FREE by using a gluten-free loaf of bread. See page 15 for recommendations of our favorite brands.

CREOLE SEASONING

GLUTEN-FREE

DIABETIC-FRIENDLY

VEGETARIAN!

Depending on what part of the country you live in, finding premixed Creole spice blends can be a challenge. So why not make your own? This spice mix is easy enough to whip up and is great for seasoning rice, meats, stews, and veggies! In fact, it happens to be the star of our Cheesy Grits-Stuffed Eggplant Rolls with Tomato Sauce on page 82. *Makes 1 cup*

3 tablespoons smoked paprika

2 tablespoons sweet paprika

2 tablespoons onion powder

2 tablespoons garlic powder

2 tablespoons dried oregano

2 tablespoons dried basil

1 tablespoon dried thyme

2 tablespoons freshly ground black pepper

1½ tablespoons cayenne pepper

1 tablespoon celery seeds

1 In a large bowl, combine the smoked and sweet paprikas, onion powder, garlic powder, oregano, basil, thyme, black pepper, cayenne pepper, and celery seeds.

2 Store in an airtight container for up to 2 months.

MEXICAN
Cornbread

 **VEGETARIAN!** The Mexican flavors Sandy grew up with shine in this recipe. The sweetness of this cornbread blends so perfectly with the southwestern spices. We love to serve it alongside most any grilled meat. *Serves 12*

1 cup (2 sticks) unsalted butter, melted, plus more for the pan

1 cup sugar

4 large eggs

1 (15-ounce) can cream-style corn

1/2 (4-ounce) can chopped green chili peppers, drained

1/2 cup shredded Monterey Jack cheese (2 ounces)

1/2 cup shredded Cheddar cheese (2 ounces)

1 cup all-purpose flour

1 cup yellow cornmeal

4 teaspoons baking powder

1/4 teaspoon salt

1 Preheat the oven to 300°F. Lightly butter a 9 x 13-inch casserole dish.

2 In a large bowl, whisk together butter and sugar until light yellow, about 3 minutes. Beat in the eggs one at a time and whisk until smooth. Stir in the corn, chilies, and cheeses.

3 In a separate bowl, combine the flour, cornmeal, baking powder, and salt. Add the flour mixture to the corn mixture and stir until smooth. Pour the batter into the prepared casserole dish.

4 Bake for 1 hour, until a toothpick inserted into center of the dish comes out clean. Let cool for 10 minutes before serving.

This dish can be made **GLUTEN-FREE** by replacing the flour with a gluten-free all-purpose mix, either store bought (see page 15 for recommendations of our favorite brands) or homemade (see page 186 for our recipe). Also, be sure to use a gluten-free baking powder.

COOK'S
Cornbread

Best made in a cast-iron skillet, this cornbread is a true Southern staple and can be served with almost any meal. It differs from our Mexican cornbread in that it is considerably less sweet. Crystal and her mom love to eat this with soup beans and a glass of buttermilk! How's that for a Southern delicacy?

VEGETARIAN!

Serves 8

Cooking spray

2 cups white cornmeal, plus more for the pan

1 teaspoon salt

2 cups boiling water

1 cup whole milk

2 large eggs

4 teaspoons baking powder

1 tablespoon unsalted butter, melted

1 Preheat the oven to 375°F. Spray an 8 x 8-inch pan with cooking spray and dust it with cornmeal.

2 In a large, heatproof bowl, sift together the cornmeal and salt. Slowly pour the boiling water over the cornmeal. Add the milk quickly, whisking constantly to avoid lumps. Add the eggs and beat well. Add the baking powder and melted butter, and beat well. Pour the batter into the prepared pan.

3 Bake for 30 to 35 minutes, or until golden brown.

This dish can be made GLUTEN-FREE by using a gluten-free baking powder.

CHICKEN
Stock

We imagine you're asking why you should make your own stock. The main reason is that

you'll get a richness of flavor in your homemade stock that you just can't buy from the store. Homemade stock has an intense chicken flavor and an unbeatable smell. While the thought of making your own stock may seem intimidating, we promise that it's not hard! In fact, it requires little attention once all the ingredients hit the pot. *Makes 2 quarts*

2 pounds chicken bones (from about 2 cooked chickens)

1 large onion, unpeeled and quartered

1 large carrot, roughly chopped

2 celery ribs, roughly chopped

1 leek, roughly chopped

2 bay leaves

2 fresh flat-leaf parsley sprigs

2 fresh thyme sprigs

5 whole black peppercorns

Salt and freshly ground black pepper

1 Put the chicken bones, onion, carrot, celery, leek, bay leaves, parsley, thyme, and peppercorns into a 5-quart stock pot and cover with cold water. Set the pot over high heat and bring to a boil. Reduce the heat to low and simmer for 3 to 4 hours. Check the seasoning after a couple of hours and season with salt and pepper to taste.

2 Remove the pot from the heat and let the stock sit for 10 to 15 minutes. Strain the stock through a fine sieve, discard the solids, and put the stock in the refrigerator overnight.

3 The next day, skim the coagulated fat off the top of the stock. If you don't plan to use your chicken stock within 48 hours, put the stock in zip-top freezer bags and freeze. The stock will keep in the freezer for up to 3 months.

BEEF
Stock

Store-bought beef stock works just fine, but—just like with chicken stock—it just doesn't compare to the homemade version. The trick with beef stock is to roast the bones first in order to achieve a nice caramelized flavor. *Makes 2 quarts*

6 pounds beef soup bones (ask your butcher for them)

2 medium onions, roughly chopped

3 medium carrots, roughly chopped

3 celery ribs, roughly chopped

1 large tomato, quartered

2 tablespoons tomato paste, thinned with 2 tablespoons water

1 garlic clove, crushed

3 to 4 fresh parsley stems, roughly chopped

½ teaspoon chopped fresh thyme leaves

1 bay leaf

8 whole black peppercorns

1 Preheat the oven to 450°F.

2 Put the beef bones, onions, and carrots in the bottom of a 9 x 13-inch casserole dish. Bake, turning occasionally, for about 30 minutes, or until the bones are very brown. Let cool for 30 minutes, and then drain the fat out of the pan.

3 Put the browned bones, onions, and carrots in a large stockpot. Pour ½ cup water into the casserole dish, and then scrape the brown bits off the bottom of the dish. Pour the liquid into the soup pot—this liquid holds a ton of flavor! Add the celery, tomato, tomato paste, garlic, parsley, thyme, bay leaf, and peppercorns. Set the pot over high heat, add 12 cups water, and bring the mixture to a boil. Reduce the heat to low. Cover and simmer for 5 hours. Strain the stock, discarding the meat, vegetables, and seasonings.

4 Let the stock cool completely. Transfer to an airtight container and refrigerate overnight. The next day, skim off all the fat that's risen to the surface. If you don't plan to use your beef stock within 48 hours, put the stock in zip-top freezer bags and freeze. The stock will keep in the freezer for up to 3 months.

VEGGIE STOCK

GLUTEN-FREE

DIABETIC-FRIENDLY

VEGETARIAN!

Unlike the longer cooking times necessary for meat-based stocks, vegetable stocks come together fairly quickly and there is no fat to skim! Making this staple is one of those things that's really easy to do, and consists of ingredients that you are likely to always have on hand. *Makes 2 quarts*

2 tablespoons vegetable oil

1 medium onion, peeled and chopped

1 medium celery rib, chopped

1 medium carrot, peeled and chopped

1 tomato, chopped

3 cloves garlic, peeled and crushed

2 bay leaves

2 fresh thyme springs

3 to 4 fresh parsley springs

3 to 4 whole black peppercorns

2 teaspoons salt

1 In a 5-quart stockpot set over medium heat, heat the oil. Add the onion, celery, carrot, tomato, and garlic and cook for about 5 minutes, or until the onions are soft and translucent.

2 Pour in enough cold water to cover the vegetables. Add the bay leaves, thyme, parsley, black peppercorns, and salt. Bring to a boil, reduce the heat to low, and simmer for 30 to 45 minutes.

3 Strain stock and let cool. Store the stock in an airtight container in the refrigerator for up to 1 week or in the freezer for up to 3 months.

CREAM OF MUSHROOM SOUP

There are some exceptions where homemade just makes good-flavor common sense. This recipe boasts a lovely, woody mushroom flavor that doesn't compare to the canned variety. It's perfect as a warm meal on a cold night or for adding to your favorite recipes, such as our Tater Tot Casserole on page 110. *Makes 3 cups*

2 quarts chicken stock, homemade (see page 192) or store bought

1/2 cup (1 stick) unsalted butter

2/3 cup chopped leeks, white parts only

1 1/2 cups white button mushrooms, chopped

1 cup all-purpose flour

1 1/2 teaspoons dried thyme

2 bay leaves

1/2 teaspoon salt

1/2 teaspoon freshly ground black pepper

1 cup heavy cream

1 In a large saucepan set over medium-high heat, bring the chicken stock to a boil.

2 In a separate large saucepan set over medium heat, melt the butter. Add the leeks and mushrooms and cook, stirring, for 8 to 10 minutes. Add the flour and thyme and cook for 2 more minutes, until the raw-flour flavor has cooked out.

3 Gradually, while whisking constantly, add the stock to the vegetable mixture. Add the bay leaves, salt, and pepper, and bring the mixture to a boil. Reduce the heat to medium and simmer gently for 30 to 35 minutes, stirring from time to time, until the soup thickens.

4 Remove the bay leaves and puree the soup in batches in a blender. (Never fill the blender more than half full.) Pour the soup through a fine strainer into a clean medium saucepan. Put the pan over medium-high heat, add the cream, and bring to a boil. Reduce the heat to low and simmer for 10 minutes. Serve hot, or cool down completely and store in an airtight container in the refrigerator for 1 week.

FREEZES WELL! **For best results, thaw cream soups in a double boiler to prevent them from burning.**

This soup can be made GLUTEN-FREE by replacing the flour with a gluten-free flour mix, either store bought (see page 15 for recommendations of our favorite brands) or homemade (see page 186 for our recipe).

CREAM OF CHICKEN SOUP

Creamed soups are often used as a base ingredient in casseroles, and cream of chicken is among the most popular of choices. Trust us when we say that making this soup from scratch and using it in recipes instead of the canned stuff will make a huge flavor difference by highlighting the freshest ingredients, and you'll be doing away with the preservatives and artificial colorings, too. This soup is fantastic as an ingredient in recipes, but don't be afraid to make it as a stand-alone dish as well. *Makes about 4 cups*

2 tablespoons vegetable oil

1 medium onion, chopped

5 tablespoons all-purpose flour

3 cups whole milk

1 cup heavy cream

2 cups roasted chicken, finely shredded (see page 200)

1 tablespoon sugar

1 teaspoon dried thyme

1 teaspoon garlic powder

1 teaspoon salt

1 teaspoon freshly ground black pepper

1 In a large saucepan set over medium heat, heat the oil. Add the onion and cook until translucent and soft, about 8 minutes.

2 Gradually stir in the flour and cook for 1 minute. Slowly add the milk and cream, stirring to prevent any clumps from forming. Cook until mixture thickens, about 5 minutes.

3 Add the chicken, sugar, thyme, garlic powder, salt, and pepper. Stir well and simmer for 10 minutes, or until the soup begins to thicken.

4 Serve hot or, if not using immediately, allow to cool completely, then store in an airtight container for up to 1 week.

FREEZES WELL! **For best results, thaw cream soups in a double boiler to prevent them from burning.**

This soup can be made GLUTEN-FREE by replacing the flour with a gluten-free flour mix, either store bought (see page 15 for recommendations of our favorite brands) or homemade (see page 186 for our recipe).

MARINARA SAUCE

Fuhgetaboutit! Marinara sauce is a great thing to have on hand at all times to make a fast and flavorful meal. Double or triple this recipe and freeze the sauce in pint-size containers. Just pull one out of your freezer, thaw and warm it, and toss it with cooked pasta to make a quick, delicious dinner. Or for a quick snack, spoon some on toasted Italian bread and sprinkle with your favorite cheese (Parmesan and mozzarella work nicely). *Makes 3 cups*

GLUTEN-FREE

VEGETARIAN!

¼ cup olive oil

4 garlic cloves, chopped

2 shallots, chopped

1 (28-ounce) can crushed tomatoes

½ teaspoon dried oregano

3 fresh basil leaves, chopped

1 teaspoon red pepper flakes

Salt and freshly ground black pepper

1 In a medium saucepan set over medium heat, heat the oil. Add the garlic and shallots and cook until the garlic starts to brown, about 8 minutes. Do not burn the garlic or you will end up with a bitter sauce.

2 Add the tomatoes with their juice, and the oregano, basil, red pepper flakes, salt, and pepper, and stir well. Bring the mixture to the boil, stirring occasionally. Reduce the heat to low and simmer gently for 25 to 30 minutes, or until the sauce has thickened.

3 If not using immediately, let cool completely and store in an airtight container in the refrigerator for up to 2 weeks.

FREEZES WELL! **This sauce will keep in the freezer for 2 months. For best results, thaw it overnight in the refrigerator.**

VERDE SAUCE

This zesty salsa gets its flavor and green hue from tomatillos. Tomatillos have a tart, citruslike flavor that works as a zingy accompaniment to our Oven-Baked Spanish Tortilla on page 57. Tip: when choosing tomatillos, smaller is better since the smaller ones have a sweeter taste. Tomatillos should be green and about the size of a large cherry tomato, but the inside is white and is meatier than a tomato. They are covered by a papery husk, which may range from the pale green to a light brown. The husks are inedible and should be removed before use. *Makes 2 cups*

GLUTEN-FREE

DIABETIC-FRIENDLY

VEGETARIAN!

8 tomatillos, husked

1 medium onion, chopped

1 jalapeño pepper (remove the seeds for less heat)

3 garlic cloves, chopped

½ cup chopped fresh cilantro

1½ tablespoons fresh lime juice (from 2 limes)

Salt and freshly ground black pepper

1 In a pot of boiling water, cook the tomatillos, onion, jalapeño, and garlic for about 8 minutes, or until the tomatillos soften. Strain and reserve the cooking liquid.

2 Put the strained veggies and the cilantro in a blender or food processor and pulse a few times. With the machine running, add the reserved cooking liquid ½ cup at a time until the sauce is the consistency of thick salsa. Add the lime juice, then season with salt and pepper to taste.

3 Transfer to a large bowl and serve immediately.

FREEZES WELL! For best results, let the salsa thaw in the fridge and allow to come to room temperature before using.

PERFECT RICE
Every Time

For even the most seasoned chefs, rice can prove to be a challenge. Yes, rice. One minute short, and it's soggy; a minute extra, it can be sticky and clumped together. Unless you want to spend your hard-earned money on a rice steamer, we suggest you follow this tried-and-true method. *Makes 3 cups*

1 cup uncooked white rice

2 cups cold water

1 teaspoon salt

1 In a 2-quart saucepan, combine the rice, water, and salt. Cover with a tight-fitting lid. Bring to a boil, then turn the heat down as low as possible. Continue to cook for 14 minutes.

2 Turn off the heat and let the rice steam in the pan for 5 more minutes. Serve immediately, or store in the refrigerator in an airtight container for up to 1 week.

ROASTED CHICKEN

GLUTEN-FREE

DIABETIC-FRIENDLY

If you are looking to save money, take the time to roast your own chicken, as it can really go a long way. Our fool-proof method makes for a delicious, juicy bird every time. After trying this traditional, scrumptious recipe, don't forget to make your own chicken stock from the chicken bones, which are rich in flavor. Talk about more cluck for your buck. *Serves 4*

1 (3-pound) whole chicken (giblets removed)

Salt and freshly ground black pepper

1 tablespoon onion powder

1 cup (2 sticks) unsalted butter

1 celery rib, roughly chopped

1 Preheat the oven to 350°F.

2 Put the chicken in a roasting pan and season generously inside and out with salt, pepper, and onion powder. Put 3 tablespoons of the butter in the cavity of the chicken. Dollop 5 tablespoons of butter on the skin of the chicken. Put the celery in the chicken cavity.

3 Bake for 1 hour and 15 minutes, or until the internal temperature reaches 180°F. Melt the remaining ½ cup of butter in a small saucepan. Baste the chicken with the melted butter and drippings. Cover with aluminum foil and let rest for about 30 minutes before serving.

That German Family
SAUERKRAUT

GLUTEN-FREE

DIABETIC-FRIENDLY

VEGETARIAN!

Some people simply don't have the patience to wait the weeks necessary for sauerkraut to ferment, but we prefer this old-school way of preparing it. The wait was actually a big part of the fun when Crystal was a kid (apparently there wasn't much to do in the north Georgia mountains). *Serves 12*

1 head cabbage, chopped

4 to 6 teaspoons pickling salt

1 Pack the cabbage into 4 to 6 sterilized quart-sized Mason jars with lids. Put 1 teaspoon of the pickling salt in each jar and cover the contents with water. Put the lids on the jars and secure the band on each as tightly as you can by hand. You might want to place your jars on a baking sheet or in a shallow dish, because during the fermenting process, the lids will loosen and juice will run down the side of the jars. This is why you don't seal them completely airtight the way you do when you are canning.

2 Store in a dry dark place to ferment for 3 weeks. Crystal's family stored it in their basement, which added to the fun (it was so scary down there!). If you do not have a basement, putting them in a pantry or covering them with a towel will work just as well.

3 The sauerkraut will keep in the refrigerator for up to 4 months.

CARAMEL SAUCE

If you have never made caramel from scratch, once you make this recipe, you will ask yourself why you waited so long. In a few easy steps, you will have created a sinfully delicious sauce. Not only is it the perfect topper for our Brownies on page 166, but it is also a great topping for ice cream and dip for fruit and chocolate! *Makes 3 cups*

GLUTEN-FREE

VEGETARIAN!

1 cup (2 sticks) unsalted butter

1 cup packed light brown sugar

¼ cup granulated sugar

¾ cup honey

¼ cup heavy cream

1 In a large saucepan set over medium-high heat, melt the butter. Add the brown sugar, granulated sugar, and honey. Bring to a boil, and cook for 4 to 5 minutes, stirring once or twice (watch carefully to avoid scorching), until the sauce begins to thicken.

2 Remove the pan from the heat and swirl in the cream until it is fully incorporated. Be very careful when adding the cream because the mixture will bubble up. Mix well and remove the pan from the heat. Use immediately, or let cool completely and store in the refrigerator for up to 3 weeks.

SPICY BLOODY MARY

GLUTEN-FREE

VEGETARIAN!

In Crystal's house, along with the salt and pepper shakers sits a trusty can of Old Bay faithfully by their side. Her boyfriend, Tim, has quite the obsession with the spice mixture and requests it on pretty much everything: meats, roasted veggies, eggs, you name it. But mostly it is reserved for Sundays when they celebrate the taste of Maryland with steamed crabs and these incredibly spiced Bloody Marys! The Bloody mixture (sans the vodka) is also the secret ingredient to our Individual Bacon-Wrapped Meatloaves (page 50). *Serves 6*

3 cups tomato juice

¼ cup plus 2 tablespoons fresh lime juice (from 6 limes)

¼ cup fresh lemon juice (from 4 lemons)

3 garlic cloves, minced

2 tablespoons Old Bay seasoning, plus more for garnish

1 tablespoon prepared horseradish

1 tablespoon Worcestershire sauce, or to taste

Salt and freshly ground black pepper

1 lime, cut into wedges

1½ cups Pepper Vodka (recipe follows) or unflavored vodka

Pickled okra, for garnish

6 celery stalks, for garnish

1 In a blender, combine the tomato juice, lime juice, lemon juice, garlic, Old Bay, and horseradish, and blend until smooth. Season the mixture to taste with the Worcestershire sauce, salt, and pepper. Refrigerate the mixture in a nonreactive container for at least 6 hours, and up to 3 days, before serving.

2 To serve, run a lime wedge around the rim of each of 6 (16-ounce) tumblers and dust with Old Bay. Fill the tumblers with ice, divide the tomato juice mix among the glasses, and top off each glass with the vodka. Garnish with the pickled okra and celery stalks and serve.

Pepper Vodka
MAKES 1½ CUPS

1½ cups vodka
4 serrano chili peppers, sliced lengthwise

Combine the vodka and peppers in a glass jar with a lid and cover tightly. Let sit for 12 to 24 hours, strain and discard the peppers, and serve.

ACKNOWLEDGMENTS

Collectively

To Jenny Alperen and Carla Glasser, the wonder twin literary agents! If anyone appreciates the balance a strong partnership brings to the table, it is us! We are so lucky to work with the Betsy Nolan Agency and two talented women who get how we operate. Thank you, Jenny, for discovering us on the telly and introducing us to Carla; with your support, there is much to look forward to. *Onward!*

If it isn't broken, don't fix it! The Queens are so thankful that we resumed our working relationship with the fine team at Clarkson Potter. You get us, and we can't thank you enough for letting us be our quirky selves. We would especially like to thank our dedicated editor, Ashley Phillips, whose wisdom and guidance is always spot-on; and the talented team that helped produce and support this book: Pam Krauss, Doris Cooper, Rica Allannic, Rae Ann Spitzenberger, Patricia Shaw, Kevin Garcia, Anna Mintz, and Allison Renzulli.

To Ben Thompson. Thank you for being someone we can truly trust and for always having our best interests at heart.

To Susan Spencer and Kate Merker with *Women's Day* magazine. The experience we have gained by working with you and your teams has made us stronger and more confident in our abilities as recipe developers and authors. Thank you.

They say a photograph is worth a thousand words, and in this case, words like *gorgeous*, *delicious*, and *mouthwatering* top the list! Thank-you to Ben Fink for gorgeous pictures and for gathering such an amazing and talented team.

Bruce Sieldel, Santos Loo, and the whole team at Hungry. We are so grateful for the experience of working with all of you. Thank you for the opportunity to grow and learn.

To Carly Pollack, our favorite nutritionist. Thank you for your knowledge and guidance. Your passion for food and health is contagious!

As we reflect on the completion of book number two, we recognize that we are extremely blessed. We know we wouldn't be anywhere without the support of our friends, family, coworkers, and casserole fans! Thank you, all, for making our lives richer.

From Sandy

To Crystal, my Co-Queen. Can you believe we have a second cookbook? Thank you for being the yin to my yang and for being so dang awesome! I love you very, *very* much.

Michael, my husband (I love saying that), you are the best.

The Pollock and the Lovitt families, for endless love and support.

And to my dear friends, who keep me laughing when I should be crying. Thank you.

From Crystal

To my favorite Casserole Queen, Sandy Pollock. After seven years of working together, the fact that our friendship is still so strong is my proudest achievement.

To Tim Tankersley and our trusty sidekick Bessie. You two help me in countless ways, but most important you make our house a home.

They say it takes a village, and trust me, it does. Thank-you to Colleen Fahey, Sarah Coker, Martha Napolillo, and Paula Simchak, for helping me use my words correctly! (And, in some cases, helping me find them!)

To Cherie Cox and all my dear friends at SicolaMartin. It is hard enough to juggle a casserole career after dark, and if it wasn't for your patience and support, I wouldn't be here.

They say that true friends are those who think that you are a good egg even though they all know that you are slightly cracked. My friends understand this statement all too well. Thank you for loving me unconditionally.

And finally, to my family. I am nothing without you all, and I love you all very much.

INDEX